I0531135

Pregnancy Survival Guide for Men

A First-Time Dad's Handbook: What to Expect from Bump to Baby. Confidently Navigate the Emotional Rollercoaster of Fatherhood and Thrive as a Supportive Partner

Dan & Dani Cambre

Budding Family Books

Copyright

© **Copyright 2023 by Dan & Dani Cambre**

Budding Family Books

The content contained within this book may not be reproduced, duplicated, or transmitted without direct written permission from the author or the publisher.

Under no circumstances will any blame or legal responsibility be held against the publisher, or author, for any damages, reparation, or monetary loss due to the information contained within this book, either directly or indirectly.

Legal Notice:

This book is copyright protected. It is only for personal use. You cannot amend, distribute, sell, use, quote, or paraphrase any part, or the content within this book, without the consent of the author or publisher.

Disclaimer Notice:

Please note the information contained within this document is for educational and entertainment purposes only. All effort has been executed to present accurate, up-to-date, reliable, and complete information. No warranties of any kind are declared or implied. Readers acknowledge that the author is not engaged in the rendering of legal, financial, medical, or professional advice. The content within this book has been derived from various sources. Please consult a licensed professional before attempting any techniques outlined in this book.

By reading this document, the reader agrees that under no circumstances is the author responsible for any losses, direct or indirect, that are incurred as a result of the use of the information contained within this document, including, but not limited to, errors, omissions, or inaccuracies.

***

MEDICAL DISCLAIMER:

This book is NOT meant to replace medical treatment or advice.

***

Russell, Hazel, and Eloise,

We dedicate this book to three of the most precious gifts bestowed upon us - the three of you. Because of you, our lives are filled with growth, adventure, and boundless joy.

Love you forever,

Mom & Dad

BONUS

Facebook Group

Become a member of a rapidly growing community of new and experienced parents by joining our Facebook Group: **Nurture Network | Support for First-Time Moms and Dads**

This group is a refuge for first-time mothers and fathers to seek advice, share experiences, and find encouragement from a community of parents on the same path as you.

FEATURES OF THE GROUP INCLUDE:

- **Self-care:** Parents often put their own needs to the side while raising a family. We will give you the boost you need to put on your oxygen mask first.

- **Mental health:** A supportive environment where members can openly discuss the ups and downs of parenting, offering emotional support and understanding.

- **Parenting Tips and Tricks:** Sleepless nights, feeding difficulties, and temper tantrums. Learn valuable gentle parenting skills.

- **Expert Advice:** Access to articles and guidance from parenting experts covering topics from bump to baby and beyond.

- **Exclusive Access to FREE Ebooks:** Geared toward parents in all walks of life.

Be sure to LIKE the **Nurture Network** page to explore other groups related to parenting and growing families!

Workbook

Scan the QR code to download your *FREE BONUS!* Inside you will find your bump-to-baby 'To Dos,' checklists, journal prompts – *& space to journal*, questions to ask your medical providers, hospital packing list, a birth plan template and other important printables referenced in this book.

Contents

About the Authors

My wife and I have been writing and publishing the *Budding Family Books* series after welcoming three gorgeous children to our home in the Pacific Northwest.

Fatherhood is challenging, but it's the most magnificent calling I've ever had. My wife also thrives as a mother and loves every moment of her journey. We had our first child over ten years ago. At the time, I was overwhelmed with fears and insecurities, but I learned along the way. We'd love to share what worked for me as an expectant dad filled with worries. My experience and knowledge will hopefully help you become the great father you're designed to be. Just know not all pregnancies and deliveries are the same, so consider this process an adventure of discovery through someone else's experience.

Today, we're a close-knit family who loves crabbing on the Oregon coast, camping, and providing opportunities for our kids to benefit from new life experiences while pursuing new hobbies, like home-steading, sports, using HAM radios, and rock-hounding. We aim to encourage our children to become their best selves while working as a team to promote our parenting experiences.

Our journey wasn't always straightforward. My wife and I had many anxieties that nearly crippled our ability to enjoy the beautiful moments of what we were blessed to have. We don't want other moms or dads to experience fear and insecurity in pregnancy or parenting. Nothing steals your joy more than lost time; losing time to fear isn't worth anything.

Through this book, we aim to buoy you up as a dad anticipating the birth of your first child. You are made for this role! We will give you the building blocks to become a rock-star dad.

Introduction

I t was a day like any other, returning home from work when it all changed—forever. Walking through the front door of our home didn't just mean returning from work that day. No, I was walking into a moment that changed my life forever for the better, but at first, there were times when it was immensely overwhelming.

I've never experienced so many emotions all at once as when Dani showed me the pregnancy stick. Two pink lines changed my world. These two pink lines brought me the best news possible, but they also came with the realization that life as I knew it would soon change and never be the same.

Of course, I was excited, but it would be foolish to deny that there were also moments of debilitating fear about whether I have what it takes to be a great dad. Questions that would cause me to lie awake at night included whether I could support my family financially, whether I'm doing enough, whether I'm doing it right, what will happen next, and what is the best thing to do right now.

My understanding of what happens during pregnancy was rather limited, I'll admit to that, but it's not entirely my fault. For the longest time—and to a large extent, it is still the case—fathers are somewhat uninformed about what occurs during pregnancy. We are just not as connected because we see the miracle happen right before us, and yet, we're excluded as our roles are just not as involved as those of moms.

You need bacon and eggs on your plate to serve a tasty breakfast. The hen committed her labor to produce the egg, but the pig sacrificed its life to produce the bacon. The way that producing breakfast influenced the lives of these two animals is just not the same, and I realized early on that I was the hen in the situation I found myself in. I wasn't sacrificing my body as Dani did with pregnancy, nor did I feel every sensation as our baby grew and moved inside. I decided that if I was going to be the hen, I wanted to be the best flipping hen you could find on the farm.

I know that comparing dads to hens can be emasculating but humor me and stick along for the ride. Soon you'll see how much clearer your role as dad becomes when we look at it from this perspective, understanding that the perfect breakfast consists of bacon AND eggs. Yes, you may sometimes feel like a mere spectator to the events changing your life too, but there is no reason for dads to remain stuck on the sideline as there is so much to do to take care of yourself, your partner, and your future family.

This all happened roughly a decade ago, and now I'm a dad to three amazing kids. Looking back on this time, I can say for sure that a lot of the mistakes I've made as a partner and a parent were due to my lack of understanding of what happens during pregnancy to our baby, my partner, and myself, on a physical and emotional level. By grasping a better understanding of these changes, I could care better for myself and Dani, and I could prepare better for the role I'm going to fulfill as a parent, but also for the one I was already in, supporting my partner through the challenges she was facing. I now know what to expect when it comes to birthing and bringing a baby home for the first time, whether it's to other siblings or as a firstborn in the family. I now know what I need to do to make Dani feel cared for and loved and how to take care of myself so that my cup isn't empty and I can provide for my family's needs, whether financially, emotionally, or physically.

One challenge we, as dads, face is our inability to define our feelings and how to manage these emotions constructively. To a large extent, this is the result of both our nature and nurture. This inability to identify and express what we are feeling often causes us to suffer in silence when matters like postpartum depression turn into a reality.

This is just one of the many facts I'll be sharing and expanding on in this book since the impact of pregnancy on fathers and how to prepare for fatherhood is widely an under-explored topic. The reality is that just as I was; many dads-to-be are underprepared for the new role they have to fulfill. By no means am I taking away the spotlight from Mom, but as a new dad, it's important to know that you must prepare yourself and commit to self-care to remain strong.

In this book, I'm sharing my experiences of every pregnancy milestone, how I prepared myself for what to expect, and how to care for your partner mentally, emotionally, and physically. Discover what you need to know and do as a couple to ensure an unbreakable bond and how to become the perfect wingman for your partner or wife when it comes to diapering, feeding, and bonding with your baby.

There is nothing wrong with feeling insecure about becoming a dad. However, what you do about your insecurities will make all the difference in the world. Are you going to be a bystander in one of the most amazing miracles that will ever take place in your life, or will you do what it takes to gain the knowledge and insights you need to be a fantastic partner and parent?

We, as dads, have no control over certain things during pregnancy, and we need to respect that. Still, there is also a lot that we can influence, make better, and be involved in, and in this book, you'll gain the wisdom to identify the difference between the two and how to influence those things best.

Are you ready to become an expert dad even before your baby is born?

Of course, you are, so let's step into the first chapter, where everything becomes clearer about pregnancy planning.

Part I

Budding Family Books

Chapter 1

From Intention to Conception

Part of being a parent is rolling with the punches, so consider an unexpected pregnancy the universe's way of helping you to learn to do that. —Heather Wittenburg

The choice to become parents is so momentous that it's often much easier to procrastinate than to take the next step. The most common excuse is that it's just not the right time, right? However, the reality is that there is never a right time, as it's challenging to know precisely what you will need to be prepared for emotionally, physically, or financially. As parents-to-be, you don't know what life will be like once your child is born. Sure, you can and should imagine how it will be, but reality may be something entirely different.

Being the dad of three kids, I can confidently say that this is the case for the birth of each child. Every child is a different person, a human being with a unique personality and needs. The birth of each of my kids brought new expectations, challenges, hopes, and blessings into our family.

All I'm saying regarding never being fully prepared or having no right time to start a family isn't to discourage soon-to-be parents who have been planning their pregnancy for quite some time. No, I'm saying this to assure parents who are expecting an unplanned pregnancy that it will be okay and that this book will offer the guidance they need too.

Planning Your Pregnancy

Whether you're thinking about starting a family or have already received the news that you're pregnant—planned or unplanned—the information I'm sharing applies to all.

Bringing a child, a new life, into this world is a serious matter and something that can place a lot of strain on both parents and their relationship, but never allow yourselves to get so entangled in planning every detail of this adventure that all the fun gets sucked out of it.

20 Questions About Your Future Family

I want us to enter this journey on a lighter note. There is hardly anything more fun, exciting, and inspiring than dreaming about your future family. Allow the following questions to guide you and your partner to dream about your future in a fun but also thought-provoking way.

1. How many children do you want?

2. Do you want a boy or a girl?

3. What names would you like to give our kids?

4. What are the things you look forward to teaching our kids?

5. What kind of life do we want to give our kids?

6. Will there be a stay-at-home parent?

7. Do we want to know our baby's gender before birth?

8. Who will be our baby's godparents?

9. What part of your upbringing did you enjoy and want your kid to have too?

10. How much of a role would grandparents play in our child's life?

11. What challenges did you face as a child and want to protect your child from?

12. How will we provide responsibilities if we both continue to work and our kids are sick?

13. What are the challenges we can prepare for in advance?

14. How will we divide getting up at night?

15. Where will our baby sleep during the first couple of months? In our room or the nursery?

16. What are the things we don't want to give up after having a baby?

17. Do we agree on our parenting approach? What would we consider spoiling, and how firm will our house rules be when our baby grows older?

18. What will we do if any blood test shows abnormalities during pregnancy?

19. How long are we willing to go without sex right before and after the birth of our baby? What can we do to stay intimate during this time?

20. Where do we want to raise our family or go for family holidays?

Working through this list can and should be fun, but it should also help you get on the same page when it comes to parenting. It offers guidance on putting a plan in place to resolve possible points of conflict now while you're both still well-rested so that you don't have to think about these things when you have both entered zombie mode due to a lack of sleep.

***

Scan the QR code to download your ***FREE BONUS!*** Inside you will find your bump-to-baby 'To Dos,' checklists, journal prompts, and other important printables referenced in this book.

***

Pregnancy Is a Time to Draw Closer to Each Other

Consider parenting a massive collaboration between yourself and your partner. Or, perhaps seeing it as a team sport is more relevant to you. A win for your team is a win for all, but it's only possible when you and your partner work together. You need to know each other's strengths and weaknesses to support each other effectively, and there's no better time to gain this knowledge than when you're expecting it as a couple.

Even though you've been together for years, parenting is an opportunity to grow closer to each other. Sadly, this stage of your relationship, and essentially your life, also holds the potential to push you apart. It's why it is so important to communicate your needs, dreams, concerns, and fears to your partner so that you can resolve these issues and get onto the same page. You don't have to agree on every little detail about parenting, but you must on the *big things* that really matter.

So, what are these *big things* you need to agree on?

The Big Things to Discuss Pre-Pregnancy

In an ideal world, you can discuss the topics listed below before you even try to become pregnant. But hey, there is often one heck of a difference between the ideal world and reality, so if your baby is already on the way, it isn't too late to find agreement on these matters.

Work

Work and finances are close to each other, and both topics have the potential to be very volatile and cause havoc in your relationship if you and your partner aren't seeing eye-to-eye. What sets work apart from finances is that having a career is about more than simply making money. It is also about considering both partners' career goals and professional aspirations.

If your partner earns less money than you, it doesn't mean that she has to put her career on hold or, even worse, let go of her professional aspirations because you're ready to start a family. No, you need to find a solution that works for both of you and your family.

It is why it is so important to have an honest conversation with your partner, stating your short-, medium-, and long-term career goals. Explain where a family will fit into these plans and how you can make this work so that you can balance family and work.

It may also mean that you need to be creative in problem-solving at times. Maybe the best solution would be for you both to continue with your careers and ask a grandparent who lives close by and is eager and able to assist in taking care of your kid while you are at work. Sometimes being creative may also mean that you can't afford that new truck you like so much, as that installment would be better spent paying for a nanny to look after your child while you're at work.

Or, perhaps your partner wants to quit her job to stay home while raising the children, and you need to find ways to balance out this loss of income. Then it may again be the truck that you'll have to sacrifice. But the beauty of parenting is that sacrifices aren't so bad because what you gain in return is so much more worth it—a family who loves you and enriches your life.

Finances

When you discuss finances, it's also important to look to added expenses that you'll have to cover as parents—now that truck may become a mere distant memory—as you have to consider the following costs in your future budget too:

- Clothing—babies need a lot of clothes, and this is surprisingly expensive considering how little fabric it needs. Consider reducing this expense by relying on hand-me-downs from friends and family.

- Childcare—if you're sending your little one to daycare or hiring a nanny. Perhaps you can rely on family or grandparents to assist.

- Food—breast milk is free, and formula isn't, but I'll say more about that soon. Consider locating a local breast milk bank. Making and freezing your own baby food is economical and healthier than store-bought options.

- Healthcare—babies tend to get sick more often, and the reality is that as a new parent, you just don't know what you're doing most of the time, so there will be more visits to the doctor and then, of course, giving birth also comes with a bill.

- Are you able to take advantage of state Medicaid healthcare? If you meet the eligibility requirements, your partner may have access to coverage during pregnancy, and your baby may have coverage for up to a year.

- Transport—are you familiar with the prices of a stroller and baby car seat, and may you need a bigger car? Browse *Facebook Marketplace* and *Craigslist* to find the next to new strollers. Keep in mind that when you purchase a second-hand car seat, it still complies with current safety standards.

- Education—daycare, schooling, or a college fund.

- A lot of miscellaneous expenses. *A lot.*

Should these expenses keep you from starting a family? Heck no! I am just giving you the full picture of what to expect so that you're not caught by surprise when neither of you has the physical, mental, or emotional capacity to think about these issues.

Feeding

Dani had the blessing of breastfeeding our first child until he was 12 months old. With our second, her supply had dried up before hitting four months. While this was a sad loss for her at the time, it was also bitter-sweet. Her supply had depleted so quickly because our daughter slept through the night at only two weeks old. While most pediatricians recommend waking the baby to nurse, ours said to take the win and relish in the 7-hour stretches of sleep that are all too often a pipe dream for most new parents.

Our daughter was born a chunky 9-pound baby and was always a stellar eater, so the doctor was never worried about her health or intake. We took her orders and took advantage of the revered sleep, and my wife could still bond with our daughter in other ways.

For many parents-to-be, breastfeeding is the ideal option, and your partner may have a dreamy image of herself sitting in a rocking chair nurturing your child. Maybe *you* imagine walking into the nursery and seeing the love of your life sitting in the same rocking chair, breastfeeding your baby. It is a beautiful image, and I totally agree that breastfeeding is a healthy option; seeing this image is a privilege. But the reality is that not everyone is great at breastfeeding. Maybe your partner isn't producing enough milk to feed your baby, and you must consider a different feeding option.

Perhaps she doesn't want to breastfeed at all as she just doesn't feel comfortable with it, or it's not practical, or simply because it can be painful at times. I've seen what breastfeeding can do to a woman's breasts, and I'll stop by saying that it looks sore. Don't force your partner to breastfeed or make her feel bad for choosing to give your baby formula if she doesn't want to breastfeed. You would never want to jeopardize the peace in your home during this special time.

Lifestyle Changes

Do you consider your current lifestyle and health optimal for raising a family? Is your partner in good health and living a balanced lifestyle, following a nutritious diet balanced with sufficient exercise to ensure her body offers a favorable environment for your baby to grow in?

Now, I want to pause here for a moment. I know that your partner is the one who is going to carry your baby, and it's important that she is in excellent health. The doctor will prescribe a prenatal supplement and others like vitamin D, folic acid, and calcium to ensure she and the baby enjoy optimal health, but it will be unfair to expect your partner to give up certain foods, make healthy lifestyle changes, quit smoking, or stop drinking if you're merely standing on the sideline commenting on her progress. If you're both smokers, then quit along with her; your baby will breathe much better in an entirely smoke-free environment. Also, consider any pre-existing medical concerns and family history on both sides to take any necessary precautionary steps. It's already here where your supportive role in pregnancy and parenting begins. Come on now - be a team player!

Struggling to Conceive?

This is such a tough one to deal with. I mean, you might have been pondering and weighing up pros and cons for months, you're finally ready to take the next step, and then month after month, ovulation cycle after another, nothing happens. Tension starts to build, and you get frustrated with yourself, the situation, and your partner. It's just such a surge of negativity you need to deal with, and it's hard. I've seen some of our friends struggle immensely to conceive, and it nearly broke up their relationship, while some family members that struggled with infertility simply drew nearer to each other while navigating the emotional rollercoaster of trying to conceive. The difference comes from how you both handle this matter.

Some good news in this regard is that some couples just take longer to conceive for no biological reason. The stats for infertility indicate 9% of all men and 11% of all women in the United States are infertile (How Common Is Infertility, 2018). It means that if you're struggling to conceive, it's more likely due to other health factors than infertility.

Risk Factors for Men

The following are all contributing factors to why men may struggle to conceive (Infertility Causes, 2020):

- Testicular cancer or treatments

- Exposure to high heat, like saunas or hot tubs, or even due to tight underwear

- Low testosterone levels can result in a low sperm count

- Injury to the scrotum or testicles

- Cystic fibrosis or other genetic disorders

- Anabolic steroids

- Undescended testicles

- Varicocele, or enlarged veins on the scrotum

- Retrograde ejaculation—when the sperm flows back into the bladder or premature ejaculation

Risk Factors for Women

The following are all factors that can cause women to struggle to conceive (Infertility Causes, 2020):

- Blocked fallopian tubes

- Kidney disease

- Celiac disease

- Abnormal menstruation

- Pelvic inflammatory disease

- Polycystic ovary syndrome (PCOS)

- Ovarian cysts or ovarian insufficiency

- Thyroid disease

- Sickle cell anemia

- Endometriosis, uterine polyps, uterine fibroids, or other uterine concerns

- Cushing's syndrome or other pituitary gland disorders

Testing for Infertility

It's normal to become negative if you've been struggling to conceive for a while (even for a short while) and still nothing has happened. Many people will likely offer the unwanted advice of *"stop stressing. The negativity will only bring you down and make it harder to conceive."*

In this day and age, we all know that stress can adversely affect your physical health; however, this is the last thing anyone would want to hear while in the trenches of infertility. It's pouring salt on a very raw wound. You have probably been through rounds of at-home ovulation kits, tracked her basal body temperature, gone down the *Google* research rabbit hole, and spent some very emotional nights wondering, *"Why me?"* If this is your experience, I urge you to take courage because there are many proactive approaches and tests you can both take to establish where each of you is on the fertility spectrum.

The idea of submitting to testing may be daunting, but it will bring you clarity, knowing what you're dealing with, and give you and your healthcare provider the necessary insights to address this concern.

Tests for Women

To determine the causes of this concern, any or a combination of the following tests will help to shed light on the challenge you're facing:

- A pelvic exam and a pap smear will identify any signs of disease.

- Transvaginal ultrasounds are another way to determine if there are any problems in the reproductive system. For this, the doctor will insert an ultrasound wand into the vagina.

- Blood tests will detect any hormonal imbalances.

- A laparoscopy is a procedure during which the doctor inserts a small camera into the abdominal area through a small incision to determine signs of uterine fibroids, scar tissue, or endometriosis.

- During a saline sonohysterogram, doctors fill the uterus with saline to improve visibility while doing a transvaginal ultrasound.

- A hysterosalpingogram is when your doctor uses injectable dye to see if there are any blockages in the fallopian tubes with an x-ray.

Tests for Men

While the list of tests for women is quite comprehensive, there are generally far fewer tests to determine infertility in men. Here we look at the following options:

- A blood test can determine testosterone levels or chromosomal abnormalities.

- A scrotal ultrasound can identify testicular problems or varicoceles.

- A semen analysis can check for sperm counts, the quality, and the mobility of sperm. While it is not the norm, in some cases, it is necessary to remove sperm with a needle from the testicles for testing.

Infertility Treatment Options

In most cases, the concerns can be treated with either surgery or medication. However, there are several options to address infertility that I want to expand on as proceeding with these options may be expensive, and you need to be on the same page as a couple before giving this expense the green light.

Intrauterine Insemination (IUI)

During this treatment, your healthcare provider places your (or a donor's) sperm directly into the uterus during the ovulation period, and fertilization takes place in your partner's body.

In Vitro Fertilization (IVF)

This refers to a method depending on greater assistance. First, the eggs are harvested and then placed with sperm in a lab dish, allowing the sperm to fertilize the eggs naturally. Then, only the fertilized eggs are transferred to the uterus. This tends to be a more expensive route to overcome infertility.

Intracytoplasmic Sperm Injection (ICSI)

During the process, a singular sperm cell is injected into several harvested eggs, and then they're transferred to the uterus. What makes this different from IVF is that here, the sperm is injected into the egg instead of being allowed to fertilize the egg by itself in the lab dish.

Assisted Reproductive Therapy (ART)

For this, couples would rely on donor eggs or sperm, or even donor embryos, and often a surrogate is used to carry the baby.

Reducing the Risks of Infertility

What can you do to avoid infertility? Well, there are certain things you can do to improve your chances of falling pregnant naturally. Still, some concerns are obviously much more complex, and no amount of healthy eating, ample sleep, or exercise will prevent infertility if it's caused by a genetic disorder, for example. Yet, the following steps will still improve the odds in your favor and keep you healthy too.

- Follow a healthy and balanced diet

- Don't smoke or use drugs

- Limit the amount of alcohol you consume

- Stay fit, but don't overdo it

- Limit exposure to toxins as much as possible

- If you've got an STD, be sure to get it treated

Just the idea of struggling with infertility is something that made me extremely nervous as I know the strain it can place on a couple. Fortunately, thanks to significant advancements in this field, there is just so much more that can be done now for couples who struggle than only a decade or two ago.

The Big Things to Discuss During Pregnancy

Let's move on to a more pleasant topic, something you need to discuss during pregnancy. This is the best time to consider your parenting style once your baby comes home.

Parenting Styles

Did you know there are 12 different parenting styles to choose from? Most parents choose a combination of styles, allowing even more options.

Let me give you a quick overview of these parenting styles:

- **Natural:** Living a relaxed outdoor lifestyle, keeping busy with outdoor activities—one of our family's favorites.

- **Traditional:** This is a more conservative approach to parenting where the parents are the authority, and children must adhere to their parent's rules.

- **Disciplined:** This is an even stricter form of parenting with definite consequences for bad behavior.

- **Intensive:** A parental style with a lot of focus on the kids to excel in life. This would mean outstanding academic performance, sports achievements, and doing well in other extra-curricular activities.

- **Child-Led:** If traditional is on one end of the spectrum, child-led would be on the opposite end. In such a household, children set boundaries for themselves, and the purpose of this type of parenting aims to raise self-sufficient kids.

- **High Achievement:** This is similar to intensive parenting, but to a greater extent, as the kids are constantly pushed to do even better and reach their highest potential.

- **Helicopter:** Parents maintain constant supervision of their kids, resembling a hovering helicopter.

- **Strict:** Follow the rules! Always!

- **Free Range:** Kids are allowed to explore the world without supervision.

- **Routine:** Somewhat like traditional parenting but at the core of this parenting style, you'll find a structure that guides kids through life and offers them security and protection.

- **New Age:** Follow the fun! Everything in this household is about having fun, and rules don't exist.

- **Negotiation:** Parents consider their kids as their equals. This is the type of parenting style that relies on lots of deep conversations to explore feelings and to offer support to every family member.

Which of these styles speak the most to you? When selecting a parenting style, both parents must be comfortable with the chosen option and have clarity as to why they've chosen this specific style. Remember, gleaning elements of multiple parenting styles can still benefit you. You also need to be sure that you both have the same understanding of what the specific style entails, allows, and prohibits to prevent any confusion or conflict later on. Being on the same page as your partner and expressing the expectations to your children ahead of time can bring you closer together and lead to a more harmonious home.

What If We Don't Agree?

Parenting styles can be quite personal, and just because you and your partner love each other or have been together a long time doesn't always mean that you share the exact same vision regarding parenting and what style(s) to follow. It's quite often the case that parents disagree in this regard. While you don't have to have all of this ironed out in the first trimester, I recommend that you reach a conclusion by the third. How do you come to a workable solution?

Talk About It

Most things in life and in relationships can be resolved through open and honest communication. This would mean that both need to state why they prefer a specific parenting style and listen to the reasoning of the other. It also means that both will have to find a golden midway with which you can agree. Please don't agree to something only to change your mind once your baby is born. This will only undermine your partner as a parent, confuse your kid, and lead to confrontation.

Set Rules as a Team

There is probably no other situation in life when it's as important to be on the same page as when raising kids. It is why you need to set rules as a team. Both need to agree that this is the best rule to benefit the family unit, bringing us to the next point too.

Be on the Same Page With Consequences

Rules come with consequences, and as much as you need to agree on the rules, you need to agree about the consequences if these rules aren't followed. Stick together even if your child looks at you all innocently. Remember who you rely on as part of your parenting team.

Have Each Other's Backs

Don't badmouth your partner to your kids. Don't even blow off steam about her toward someone else when your kids are within hearing distance. Even if you think they can't hear you believe me, they do. Children have supersonic hearing whenever you don't want them to be listening in. It feels like only when you want them to hear that they struggle to listen. Just refrain from saying bad things about your partner—always. This will give your children a sense of stability and love in the home.

Be Open to Change

Family situations change, the environment you're in may change, and your children grow older, bringing about change, which means that you need to be open to updating the rules too. When it comes to adjusting the rules for your family, you need to do it in collaboration with your parenting team member—your partner.

When you have more than one child, you will quickly realize that different children respond better or worse to different parenting styles. Again, communication is *key*. Ensure you and your partner remain on the same page and find the best balance to parent your kids equally.

FAQs

Q: How successful are fertility treatments?

A: Roughly 90% of all fertility treatments lead to success. It's important to consider factors like your age, health, and if there are any underlying medical concerns. These factors will impact your success.

Q: Will my insurance pay for infertility treatment?

A: Health insurance policies vary regarding the finer details, and while some will pay for this type of treatment, it doesn't mean that all do. So, it's best to check with your insurance provider first. It's also recommended to consider state laws, as some states require that employers pay for certain types of infertility treatments.

Q: When should I start saving for my child's college fund?

A: It is always best to start earlier rather than later. The best time would be to start when your child is born, but if you can't do it straightaway, you can always begin saving later on too. It only means that you'll have to save more per month.

Checklist

The following checklist is a list of topics to address with your partner before and during pregnancy that will help you stay on track as a supporting partner.

1. How many kids do we want to have?

2. Will both of us continue to work, or will one be a stay-at-home parent?

3. Who can we rely on for support? Grandparents, family, or friends.

4. Will we hire a nanny or send our kid to daycare?

5. When and how much do we want to save for a college fund?

6. What changes should we make to our budget to ensure comfortable living?

7. If we struggle with infertility, how far are we willing to go with treatments before giving up or looking at other options?

8. What is the alternative if we give up? Adoption? Fostering?

9. What parenting style(s) have we decided on?

10. Why have we chosen this type of parenting?

Conclusion

How does Darth Vader like his toast? On the dark side.

A poor joke always lightens the mood after such serious information. So, I hope it gripped a giggle or at least a good eye roll. Plus, it's time to start building that 'dad joke' repertoire for when your little one arrives.

Remember, you and your partner might have a successful conception, and when that happens, bless both of you. Your lives are about to change, and it's time to see how to know what you can do as a dad.

In the next chapter, we'll explore how you can care for yourself during pregnancy and parenthood. Remember, you can only pour from your cup and support your partner and family when you've ensured your cup is full too.

Chapter 2

Nurturing Yourself While Expecting

I need to start caring about myself if I'm going to be a proper father. —Shannon Hoon of Blind Melon

I grew up on a farm. It was a fantastic environment where my brother and I could run wild. We both enjoyed being outdoors and would often get so involved in playing our games that we would completely forget about the *mad hen*. That is what we called one of our chickens. Some days this hen—a rusty red one with a few white feathers towards her tail—would ignore us completely. But on other days, she would be miserable and chase us across the farmyard - like something you'd expect from a rooster. As boys of about six and five, we only had one escape from the hen's animosity: through the backdoor of our home. Nobody knew why she would be so miserable on some days, but since we never knew what her mood would be, we were always somewhat wary of her, warned each other when we saw her, and in general, tried not to cross her way.

 Why am I sharing this story? I guess the image of me constantly working towards being the best hen I can be is still stuck in my mind and probably will be forever, but it's not the only reason why I think about this *mad hen. Nope, there's another lesson to learn here.* See, the hen wasn't in a bad mood every day, but since we never knew in what mood she'd be in, we were scared of her every day.

The same happens in relationships. If you are moody, snapping at your loved ones on some days, you're effectively making them weary or hesitant to reach out to you on all the other days, too. If you've shown them that you have an unpredictable temperament, they'll hesitate to reach out to you and strengthen your bond. It doesn't matter that you're moody because you're tired or stressed or for any other valid reason. Nope. Your loved ones will remember how you made them feel when you snapped at them for wanting your attention.

For now, it may only still be your partner facing the brunt of your mood, which is already bad enough. But what about when your child is born? Do you want to offer your unborn baby childhood memories infused with fear and uncertainty, as they may never know what mood you'll be in?

As I aspired to be the best hen in the pen, I realized early on for me to be in a good mood and to be able to be there for my wife and, later on, my kids, I needed to take care of myself first. It's the only way I could take care of them, too, the way I *wanted* to care for them—unconditionally.

Your Hormonal Changes

Typically, we associate hormonal changes with being a female problem, right? Well, hold your horses because research indicates that men also experience significant hormonal and physiological changes during pregnancy as well. Now, don't many of the challenges you've been facing suddenly make sense?

Researchers found that it's especially fathers who are emotionally involved in their relationship and the pregnancy whose testosterone levels drop while prolactin and vasopressin levels increase. Prolactin is a hormone surging in women after breastfeeding and in men after a sexual climax, while vasopressin is a hormone responsible for bonding (Boyle, 2013).

We also now know that estradiol levels decline in prenatal dads. Estradiol fulfills different roles in men and women. In men, this is the hormone that ensures libido, sperm production, and erectile function (Ramasamy et al., 2016). When these levels drop, you will likely be less interested in sex and more focused on intimacy and caring for your partner. I know this can be a confusing time, but it's a natural state for dads to be in while their partners are pregnant.

These hormonal changes can persist for a while after birth, and the more dads are involved in caring for their babies and interacting with their kids, the more they'll experience similar emotional rushes as mothers usually do when looking after their young. It also appears that the greater the decline in these hormones, the bigger the father's involvement in caring for the newborn after birth (Edelstein et al., 2016).

Dads and Postpartum Depression

Then there is also the concern with postpartum depression (PPD)—again, a concern usually linked with moms. This assumption is best to let go of, as studies indicate that just over 14% of dads suffer from anxiety. One out of every 20 dads-to-be experiences postpartum depression, and that number doubles after the baby is born (Happity, n.d.). The number of men suffering from *prenatal depression* is a whopping 1 out of 10 (Horsager-Boehrer, 2021). This shocked me when I initially became aware of this research as it is a widely under-published topic. While some men may not like the idea of themselves experiencing hormonal changes, I know that this is a nugget of wisdom that would help a lot of dads-to-be resolve conflicts in their relationship during pregnancy and beyond.

This decline in your mental and emotional state can be rooted in a range of causes. Sometimes it's the mentioned hormonal changes that can cause you not to feel yourself, but it can also be your partner's depression that impacts you. Dani experienced fairly severe prenatal and postnatal depression with our third child. While anxiety wasn't a new concept to her, we were surprised by the massive low she experienced with this pregnancy. We were both elated to be pregnant, but the emotional challenge of depression completely rocked us. I felt lost and confused about how to help her through her struggles. I also didn't want to complain about my own personal challenges for fear of adding too much to her emotional plate. I learned, though, that open communication can only help the relationship. Over time I learned to talk more openly about my feelings. This has helped me recognize and identify bouts of anxiety I never realized I had, and my wife and I help walk each other through those difficulties.

Many reasons can lead to depression in dads. Perhaps you're feeling disconnected from your partner and baby, like you're the third wheel in the relationship, even before your baby is born. However, the best way to overcome these challenges is to share them with your partner. As much as you're there to support her, she'll be there to support you, after all, you're a team, and that is what team members do for each other.

Sleep deprivation is another huge contributing factor impacting your mental and emotional state. It can be so easy to fall into a habit of lying awake at night and worrying about the future, pondering whether you'll be a good dad or make enough money to take care of your family. There are just so many things that keep your mind busy, and as long as you keep staring at the ceiling instead of getting sufficient shuteye, you'll be tired the next day. Eventually, your exhaustion will reach a point where everything might seem too much to handle.

So, what now? If this is the reality of your current situation, what can you do about it?

How to Take Care of Yourself

Before you can take care of your partner or your relationship, you need to take care of yourself.

By no means do I suggest that you do exactly what I did to sustain my mental health during three pregnancies and ever since. No, my wish is that you find guidance on what to do and encouragement to prioritize your mental health so that you never become the *mad hen* in your home.

Actively Seek Mental Health

How do you see your role as a partner and future parent? Do you consider yourself to be the superhero coming to everyone's aid? That is quite a pair of pants to fill, and the likelihood is that you'll fail over and over in your attempts if you don't bring your best game to the playing field. Your best game depends on a healthy and clear state of mind. So, if you feel things are getting too much, take a step away to clear your head. Take a walk or just get some fresh air. Sometimes a quick breather is all you need to pull yourself together and give your family the best version of you. If you feel lost on your own or stepping away doesn't help, then be sure to communicate this with your partner so that she can be sensitive to your needs.

Find Your Support Network

There is an African proverb saying that *if you want to go fast, go on your own, but if you want to go far, you need to go together*. When you're becoming a father, going far is your only option. So, pick a good crowd of people to share this journey with you. The best crowd is usually also fathers facing the same challenges you do. These guys can be your friends or family, or you can join a more formal support group for dads. By now, you'll find these groups probably in most big cities, but if there are none where you live, start one. You'll be surprised to discover how many dads will sign up for this support. If getting together isn't your jam, simply joining a new dad or parenting group on *Facebook* can give you access to a support group of men going through similar life experiences.

Daily Mental Health Practices

One of the best mental health practices for sustained wellness during pregnancy and after birth is to do something you enjoy daily. Pausing for a mental health break doesn't always come naturally to most men, so think about what you like doing that makes you feel happy and content. I can also tell you that the best way to turn this practice into a habit is to  give your partner the same opportunity. Both parents need to take time to do something just for themselves. Maybe it's just taking a nap or a quick jog in the park. My wife likes to take a long soak in an Epsom salt bath, and I enjoy sitting by myself on our back porch with my feet up on the propane fireplace. Just make sure you do it and that you do it for yourself, and give your partner the time to do the same to sustain her mental health too.

Know Your Value

Sure, you won't be carrying your baby for roughly 40 weeks, and you won't be the one going through the birthing process, but you matter too. Over recent years, studies again emphasize dads' vital role in their kids' lives.

When dads are involved in their children's lives, these kids turn out to be more ready for school, have a better vocabulary, show strong social skills, and do better with emotional development than when dads are absent (*New Dads and Mental Health — 8 Tips to Stay Healthy*, 2022).

Go Easy on Yourself

Why are you so hard on yourself? Do you think you might lack the skills to be a dad? It seems that so many dads think that mothers have a natural maternal instinct but that they have to earn some kind of qualification to be a dad. If this is what you're thinking, stop right now. Just stop it. What do your kids need from you? To be happy, to love their mother and love them, to be there for them, and to be yourself. That is all there is to it. So, as long as you take care of these things and you most likely have lots of experience in doing this, you'll be fine. See, you can give yourself a break!

Maintain Balance in Your Life

Sometimes, it can feel like talking about your baby and thinking about the pregnancy and your unborn child is consuming your entire life. Becoming a parent doesn't mean that you have to lose yourself. Becoming a parent is something you're doing because you want to enrich your life with this experience that can't be compared to anything else. To keep yourself from feeling this way, it will help to learn new skills that may restore balance in your life. You're human, a person with friends, extended family, interests, and a pre-pregnancy life. Now that you're expecting, you may have to find a different time to do certain things, but it's still important to do things that make you happy and help you maintain a balanced life.

Learn About Your Baby

The more you know about your baby and his or her development, the better prepared and more involved you'll feel in the process. In the next chapter, I'll be sharing *so many* nuggets of wisdom and information about what is happening during the first trimester. Read up on it and stay informed for your own benefit and to be able to make a valuable contribution to any pregnancy conversations or milestones.

Give Support to Others

There is nothing that comes close to the emotional boost we get when helping someone else out. The more you help others, the better you'll feel. Doing these things give you a sense of purpose and feeling appreciated. It also allows you to connect to others. These are all benefits you can enjoy from volunteering. Is there a place in your community that needs volunteers? A place where you can help out and give back some support to others? See how you can become part of it.

Be Mindful

Maybe you've heard the term before but don't really grasp what it entails. It can so easily be misunderstood as a method exclusively practiced in retreats where you merely sit with your legs folded while smelling the flowers all day. It's not. Just be more aware of what you're feeling. If something is off, identify what it is that you're feeling and why you're feeling this way. Also, take note of sensations in your body. It will boost your mood and even leave you feeling more confident to make the most of this beautiful but slightly daunting time ahead. Sharing these realizations with your partner can bring you closer together and help you get to know each other even deeper.

You can do better as a future dad and a loving and supportive partner when you have an open mind.

Keeping Up the Relationship

Are you familiar with the phrase, *happy wife, happy life*? You may or may not agree with this, but what I can say with certainty is that your life will surely be much happier if you're *both* happy in your relationship. To have a healthy relationship, you need to do your bit to support your partner's happiness. I agree you can't *make* someone else—not even your partner—happy. Everyone needs to do it for themselves. But there are many things you *can* do to maintain this happy state, even though we can all be so easily guilty of doing things or failing to do things that will cause this state to crumble.

What *is* the current state of your relationship? There's hardly a better time to ensure you sustain a supportive relationship than during pregnancy, as this relationship will set the foundation of your family life in the years to come. But first, the following three questions will get you thinking about the state of your relationship:

1. Am I giving my wife enough attention? (She is more likely to provide you with an accurate answer to this question.)

2. Am I good enough for my partner?

3. What if my feelings for my partner change during this journey?

Now, as you probably have a pretty good idea of the current state of your relationship, let's see why relationships can be so much harder to maintain during pregnancy. One word—*hormones*. Yep, the increase and changes in hormonal levels you both are experiencing are undoubtedly the main contributing factors to the volatile emotional state you've been experiencing in your relationship. At times, it may feel as if you just don't know your partner at all anymore, and this in itself can cause uncertainty and a feeling of insecurity in the relationship.

Hormones amplify every emotion, resulting in higher highs and much worse lows. It's a time of increased vulnerability, causing a spike in anxiety. I'm not going to sugarcoat it – this can sometimes be a tough ride. But it's all much better when you have a happy and healthy relationship that binds you and your partner together. Without this support, you and your partner are far more likely to feel anxiety and stress about evolving from a couple to becoming parents.

Some possible friction points in your relationship are that one may feel the other isn't as interested in the pregnancy as they are, feeling physically sick or tired, feeling the pinch of financial pressure, being anxious about your ability to be great parents, the lack of intimacy and concerns over the fading desire to be intimate from a partner, or maybe you're being overly protective of your pregnant partner, and she feels like you suffocate her.

I know, without a doubt, that the best way to address these concerns is to talk it all out. Have a long heart-to-heart. It's also essential to have consistent comforting, and reassuring bouts of communication during which you express your hopes, fears, and expectations about life as a parent. This is when you can state the support you need and listen to your partner's needs in order to support her effectively.

You know, it's often the case that if we only listen to what our partners say and give them the support they need, relationships will be far less turbulent. A relationship becomes much less cumbersome and time intensive if we just love our partners how they want to be loved.

If all fails and you feel like you don't know how to move forward from the situation you're in, don't hesitate to call in professional help. Seeing a professional doesn't mean that your relationship is failing. Not at all. It means that you're willing to do what it takes to make it great again.

What can you do to improve the state of your relationship? Again, the following are all suggestions to get your mind going, and they are things that worked for us. However, in the end, you need to determine what it is that your partner needs, either by talking to her or by going to see a professional to serve as a guide along this journey.

Keep on talking about your dreams, hopes, expectations, responsibilities, and preparations. Consider these to be your *team talks*, the conversations that don't only keep the progress going but also team spirit alive.

- What are you dreaming about for yourself as a parent?

- What skills or passions do you have that you hope you can pass on to your child?

- What activities would you want your little one to be involved in?

- How will you divide responsibilities in and around the house now and after bringing your baby home to ensure you both enjoy a balanced life?

- What responsibilities does each of you like to take care of?

- Who is in your support network? Or who can you call to babysit on short notice?

- Will you go for antenatal classes?

- How are you planning to birth this baby?

The *4 Cornerstones* of a Happy and Healthy Relationship

What are the four cornerstones?

- **Actively listen** to each other. It means that you both remain mentally present when in conversation. Listen to what the other person is saying, the tone they use, mannerisms and facial expressions, as well as the gestures or non-verbal sounds they make to ensure you entirely comprehend what they're saying. It's easy to start thinking about your response long before the other person is even done talking.

- **Brainstorm** solutions to your challenges and ideas to overcome obstacles. When you work together to find solutions, it brings you closer. Then you'll truly experience what it means to work as a team and become more comfortable relying on the other person's strengths and understanding their weaknesses, knowing when you should step up for the sake of your team.

- **Negotiate** to find solutions. Sometimes you need to negotiate with outside parties, like finding a suitable time for a family gathering that will keep your partner's needs in consideration while still showing kindness toward the host inviting you. Other times you need to negotiate with each other to find a solution that makes you both happy.

- Lastly, the big C—**compromise.** Yes, sometimes you can't get exactly what you want, as that might not be the best solution for your relationship. Like when you had to sacrifice buying the truck of your dreams as it was just not an expense serving your partner or future family.

When you use these four cornerstones, you can turn conflict situations into opportunities to build your relationship constructively. Lastly, but still so important—accept each other for who you are. This means taking your differences into consideration, or in other words, *loving each other warts and all!*

I am not much of a dancer, but I've admired Dani performing the West Coast Swing with her dad at family parties and weddings. Although I don't participate, I do know that if you don't pull your dancing partner close enough to you, it can be tough to maintain the same rhythm. What you're going through isn't much different. You need to spend time with each other, pulling each other close, and be sure you continue dancing at the same pace and following each other's rhythm and movements. If not, you can forget about dancing gracefully, and it may as well just be two people shaking things out while standing too close to the other causing regular bumps or stepping on toes.

Keep the romance alive. Do you know how sexy it can be to have this romantic fling with your pregnant partner? Be spontaneous and surprise her with something she'll like. Please, don't plan a romantic camping trip because *you* love camping (although Dani loves camping). Consider her needs too, and that she might be mentally and physically drained during the first trimester, while morning sickness can be a huge headache too. Would you like to camp feeling like that? Rather spoil her with something she'll feel comfortable doing in that specific trimester.

Have as many date nights as possible since you will soon need to pay a babysitter just to take your partner to dinner. A romantic dinner can also very easily be served at home. Spoil her with a home-cooked meal. Heck, even beans on toast can be a romantic meal in candlelight. In the end, it's the idea that counts.

Movies, dancing, game nights, going to the drive-in, taking long walks in nature, and recreating your first date, are all amazing ways to keep the romantic flame alive.

This brings me to intimacy. Intimacy and sex aren't the same. When you're intimate, you immerse yourself in that close bond with your partner. You draw close to each other through small acts of kindness and caring, like when you rub her feet, hold hands, cuddle, or give an unexpected kiss on the forehead.

Do things without being asked. Ask questions to stay updated on how she feels and needs, and learn how you can help her. Stay emotionally attentive by listening to her when she needs to talk and comforting her when she needs to cry. Run her a bath, make her comfortable, and never forget to tell her how gorgeous she is. Even if you forget everything else I've said to this point, remember this. Just imagine what it must feel like when your body undergoes all these changes. Then you'll understand why it's so important to receive confirmation from your partner, the person you love, that you're still amazingly beautiful in their eyes. Her body is doing marvelous and powerful things.

Does it sound like you'd be doing all the work? First of all, remember that you're the hen, and she's the pig - but don't call her that! She is the one sacrificing far more of herself; she undoubtedly deserves to be cared for in the best possible way. Secondly, your mental, emotional, and physical wellness also benefits from investing time and effort into your partner and the health of your relationship. So, it's a win-win for the two of you.

Manage Your Physical Wellness

Now that your baby is on its way, you're bound to feel more stress placing a toll on your physical health. While your partner needs to sustain her overall health and wellness, you can also benefit from making a few vital changes to improve your health and wellness.

Change your eating habits to include more fresh, nutritious food and cut down on snacks, treats, and fried and processed foods.

Make sure you sleep as much as you can pre-birth, as sleep will become something you treasure afterward. If your partner is sleeping more than you, it is fine. Her body is busy building a little person, and that is exhausting. Support her in this and help her to get as much sleep as possible. My wife has a sticker on her water bottle that reads, "*If you love me, let me sleep.*" From one parent to another, I can attest that this is sage advice.

Remain active and help your partner stay active for as long as she can as well. Physical activity releases feel-good hormones boosting the mood. One fun way to stay active during pregnancy is with prenatal couples yoga. This isn't only a way to stay fit and flexible, but it also builds your bond, improves communication, increases the support you receive from each other, and can help you to feel more part of the pregnancy rather than a mere observer on the sidelines.

FAQs

Q: How can I be sure I am ready to support my partner during labor?

A: Talk to your local hospital to see if they offer any classes or just to take a tour through the labor and delivery area. Read up as much as you can about labor and delivery to know what to expect and how you can support your partner during this time.

Q: How active should we be to support a healthy pregnancy?

A: A healthy pregnant woman needs roughly two and a half hours of moderate-intensity aerobic activity weekly.

Q: What are some examples of how I can keep our intimacy alive when lovemaking becomes more challenging?

A: Think back to the time when you were first dating. Her qualities you noticed then were the things that attracted you to her. You'll be able to rely on these skills to maintain the closeness between the two of you. Flirt with her, cook together, have long conversations, look into each other's eyes, run errands together, hold hands, start a DIY project together, or take time apart to connect again afterward.

Checklist

The following checklist will keep you on track to ensure your cup is full enough that you can support your partner, aid in your own mental health, and sustain your relationship with ease:

1. Can I identify the emotional changes I'm experiencing?

2. Who is in my support network?

3. What can I do to maintain balance in my life?

4. What have I learned this week about the progress of our baby?

5. How would I like to surprise my partner with a romantic gesture?

6. Are we going for prenatal classes?

7. Have we compiled a to-do list for baby-proofing our home?

8. What can we do to remain active and have fun together while doing so?

9. Have I told my partner that she is beautiful today?

10. Have I told her how much I love her today?

***

Pro Tip: The questions and journal prompts are included in your BONUS workbook!

***

Conclusion

What did the two pieces of bread say on their wedding day? It was loaf at first sight.

You need a good laugh (or eye roll) once in a while and reminders that you're doing great. Stop doubting yourself, and don't allow negative thoughts about your partner or your feelings to distract you from this beautiful journey. It's temporary. So, instead, let's discover ways you can master fatherhood.

Chapter 3

Embrace the 1st Trimester With Confidence

You do a lot of growing up when you're pregnant. It's suddenly like, yikes! Here it is, folks. Playtime is over. —Connie Fioretto

L earning that you'll be a dad soon is one of those moments when you're flooded with emotions. The most predominant ones are often excitement, gratitude, and joy. But these feelings are also tainted with a bit of stress, caused by the uncertainty of whether you'll be a great parent, whether you'll be able to meet the financial needs of your new family, and if your child will be healthy.

Things to Do in the 1st Trimester

The first 12 weeks of pregnancy are referred to as the first trimester, and it's pretty normal to learn that you'll be a father only a couple of weeks into your first trimester. This stage can feel like it slips by rapidly. So, let's jump in to see what you need to get done during this period, what can help to make you feel more included in the pregnancy, and how you can best support your partner.

Find a Practitioner

Birth is a wonderful but nerve-racking process for which you may never feel entirely prepared. It's why you would want to have professionals on your team to make this as easy as possible for your baby, your partner, and yourself. It can be an immensely powerless feeling when you see what your partner is going through, and you can do nothing to make it any better for her. It's why it is crucial to find the right person for you, as a couple, to help you through this process. The typical options are to go with a doula, midwife, or doctor (or a combination of the three). When considering your options, remember that there is no right or wrong person to have by your side. It's all about finding someone with skills and expertise you trust and who makes you both comfortable.

What are the ins and outs of each? Let's see.

Obstetrician

An obstetrician, or OB, is a doctor with medical expertise in pregnancies and birth. OBs are by far the preferred choice for many women as this expert will continuously monitor the progress of your partner and baby during pregnancy. They offer advice, offer health support, and run the necessary tests to determine any existing congenital disabilities. They come with an entire support team of nurses and other doctors and at times, will even have a midwife by their side. Obstetricians are also capable of performing cesarean sections if needed.

Midwife

There are many countries where the midwife is the main support provider during birth. A Certified Nurse Midwife or CNM—also often referred to as a midwife—makes a much greater contribution to your pregnancy than merely being there for the birth. Getting a CNM on your team means you access a treasure of wisdom concerning your partner's reproductive health. These professionals also provide care during pregnancy; they can take care of gynecological check-ups, help with family planning, and even offer support for postpartum depression. The birthing experience when having a midwife by your side may involve less technology and fewer medications. Having a midwife offers a more natural birth, and while they will refer you to an OB if needed, research indicates that births where midwives are present, bring about fewer traumas (McQueen, 2023). Always choose a *certified* midwife to have peace of mind about their abilities and training. Check with your medical insurance if they'll pay for the service of a midwife. Most do, but not all.

Doula

Also called childbirth assistants, doulas are specially trained to provide comfort and support during labor and delivery. A doula often acts as a liaison among the practitioner, nurses, and the parents-to-be. Some doulas will also provide at-home assistance after the baby is born. A midwife or doctor always accompanies a doula. Their main purpose is to ensure a spiritual, holistic connection and to serve as a communication channel between you and your medical team. A doula offers support, and as the word means to serve, it's pretty evident that they are there to cater to your partner's needs. A doula can make the entire process less stressful. They concentrate on more natural birthing experiences with fewer medical interventions. Some insurance companies will even pay for a doula, so check with yours if this is possible.

Antenatal Classes

There are real benefits to attending antenatal classes. These are fun groups where you'll meet other parents who are often also expecting their first-borns. These people share the same expectations and fears as you do, and they can quickly turn into an extension of your support network. During these classes, you'll learn how to look after your baby and correct feeding methods. You'll get advice on drafting your birthing plan while also getting support on staying healthy. Many classes are held at the hospital where you plan to deliver and offer tours of the birthing room and facilities.

You'll learn everything you need to know about the birthing process in these classes and how to care for your baby during those first couple of days and weeks when they're still so tiny.

Most antenatal classes only start from around 8 to 10 weeks before birth, but it's a good idea to decide now if you'll be going and where you'll attend these classes. As previously mentioned, most hospitals offer antenatal classes, but you can also ask your OB or other parents about other classes you can attend.

Making the Announcement

When should you make it public that you're expecting a baby? We were super excited and just wanted to shout it from the rooftops, but then there was also that bit of uncertainty gnawing at our happiness. You know, those what-if questions. What if something goes wrong? What if we lose the baby? The reality is that most miscarriages happen during the first 12 weeks of pregnancy. How do you handle sharing such dismally sad news with your loved ones after you've just shared your great news with them? Not only would you have to deal with your own disappointment and sorrow, but also that of your partner, and then do you really want to expand on the possibility of heartache for even more people? Wouldn't it be easier to get through the high-risk time and only then get everyone's hopes up? This is, of course, one way you can look at it, but there is another perspective that is worth exploring too.

What if the worst happens, and you've already told everyone you love about your great news? If this is the case, you're far more likely to get the necessary emotional support from your loved ones during this time. If you haven't told them about the pregnancy, you'll most likely also not share your sad news, and this can be a very lonely place to find yourself.

But at the end of the day, it's a very personal decision to make, and the only two people who need to be on the same page here are you and your partner.

However, it's not only news you need to share with your loved ones; at some point, you'll also need to tell your employer —when it's your partner's employer, preferably before she starts to show. Again, I want to highlight that there is no guideline set in stone about when to tell your employer about your pregnancy, but you'll most likely want to take some parental leave, and for that, you need to inform your employer in advance. A great guideline is to wait until the end of the first trimester, as that will give you more certainty about the road ahead while leaving enough time for your employer to make arrangements regarding who will take care of your responsibilities while you're gone.

When it comes to sharing the news with your colleagues, the guidelines for you will be somewhat different than for your partner. She'll have to share this news sooner as they may notice she has morning sickness or need to take time for doctor appointments. She's also going to be extremely fatigued during this time. You don't have any of these challenges to face at work and can wait until you're ready to share the news. It all depends on how close you are to your coworkers.

What about friends struggling to get pregnant or even those who have lost a baby? Can you tell them? I know it can be hard to share your positive news with someone you care about when you know it's a sensitive topic to them. But the best advice I can give is to share this news with them privately. Maybe tell them first and do it in a manner that makes it evident that you respect their feelings and share their heartache but still want them to be part of this journey you're on. Mostly, it's the case that they'll be very happy for you and excited about your good news; they may just be more reserved in expressing their excitement. Once you've done this, you can share your news freely without any reservations, as long as you and your partner agree on when you'll start telling everyone about your baby.

Find A Pediatrician

The last time I heard the word pediatrician was when my parents took my younger brother to see one, and I couldn't even remember the doctor's name. Dani and I were also one of the first couples in line to have a baby in our families and our circle of friends, so word-of-mouth referrals were slim. If you find yourself in a similar position, the following pointers will direct you to find the right person for the job.

7 Points to Consider

1. Is the office conveniently located? Your baby will need to see the pediatrician a couple of times per year—multiple times during the first year—and you don't want to travel to where there is a lot of traffic or parking is hard to find. Also, pick someone near your home.

2. Did your OB-GYN recommend the pediatrician? If you're completely lost when it comes to making this choice, ask the doctor you already trust and who knows you, your OB-GYN, to recommend someone.

3. Will the pediatrician be the first person to check up on your baby after birth? Not all pediatricians choose to visit their newest patients just after birth, but some do. I've felt that having someone with such commitment on board when this new journey started could only be beneficial. Know that in most hospitals, a pediatri-

cian will be on staff or on-call, so if yours is unavailable, your baby will still have the care required before discharge.

4. What are the doctor's credentials? In the US, not all family doctors are pediatricians. Why does this matter? To become board certified, a pediatrician must complete additional courses and training that give you the certainty that they are professional, have advanced field knowledge, and excel in patient care. It also often means that they have excellent communication skills; while this may not seem important yet, believe me, you will want someone who can help you understand what may be wrong when your baby isn't feeling their best and to quell your partner's and your worries.

5. Does the pediatrician come recommended? Just because someone may come highly recommended by a family member or friend shouldn't leave you feeling obliged to rely on their medical expertise, but it does help if they come with positive feedback.

6. Does the practice's routine operations align with your needs? What are the practice's operating hours? How do they treat emergencies? How long do you need to wait for an appointment? What is their plan when you need them over a weekend? Or late at night? Children, especially when still very young, don't only get sick or develop a high fever between the hours of nine and five. Oh no! This can happen any time of day or night, and you don't want to be caught in this situation without being able to get your child to a doctor. Become familiar with the off-hour standards and whether or not they have an on-call doctor to speak to.

7. Did the introductory visit go well? If you plan to use a certain professional as your pediatrician, absolutely pay them a visit. Again, just because someone comes highly recommended doesn't mean that their personality suits yours. Only make the final call after

you've met in person.

7 Questions to Ask Your Pediatrician

What do you discuss with your pediatrician during your introductory visit? The following seven questions can guide this conversation, ensuring you get all the necessary answers.

1. How long have you been a practicing pediatrician? You need to determine their level of experience.

2. How long does a check-up usually take? This will help you determine if the doctor allows enough time for a thorough examination.

3. Do you have a call-in policy? If this is the case, you'll know how hard it may or may not be to reach the doctor (or on-call doctor) by phone.

4. Does your office keep sick and healthy children apart? Some pediatrician's offices keep children who are sick apart from those who are only there for check-ups to prevent the spread of disease.

5. What is their opinion about vaccinations? Determine how they feel about vaccinations to see if they differ from your beliefs. Also, find out why they have a specific opinion about vaccines and what facts and research they base their convictions on.

6. Are you part of a group practice? This will help you understand who you can call when your doctor is absent.

7. What are your fees, and what insurance does your practice accept? Unexpected doctor visits can be expensive, and you need to know how you'll be able to accommodate this expense in advance. In the US, well-child visits have no copay because it's considered

preventative care covered by most insurance. Always thoroughly review your insurance coverage.

Making Life Easier for Your Partner

It's important to remember that even though your partner may not show that baby bump yet, her body is very busy creating a new life, and she can do it with a bit of a break. So, when you're around, help out, especially without being asked. Or, let her know that she can rely on you to take care of certain things and to leave them so you can take care of them when you return. The golden rule is, of course, to do as promised and not make her wait to get these things done. I still have yet to come across anyone — man or woman — who would willingly wait around until you finally do as promised.

Do the heavy lifting in the house or anywhere else you go. It's not good for her or your baby to face the risk of injury when she picks up unnecessarily heavy stuff.

Do some research with her to see how you can improve your lifestyle to live a healthier life. As mentioned in the first chapter, these changes could include taking supplements, starting an exercise routine, and eating a healthy and nutritious diet. You can also lead by example while constantly supporting her in making these changes. Practice what you preach. If you make any suggestions about your partner's lifestyle, then follow your own suggestions too. These can be suggestions like quitting drinking, smoking, and taking any recreational drugs.

You can also give her a breather. She'll feel severe fatigue during the first trimester, and while she might want to keep up the pace she is used to—and she will most likely too—it will be much harder for her. So, come on, man, don't let her ask for help, don't let her struggle or let her get so tired that she becomes irritated, snappy, or angry caused by sheer exhaustion. Jump in and help her. Cook a meal, do loads of laundry. You can also bond with her by doing these tasks together.

However, it's not only the physical load of house chores that you can share but also the mental load you both may experience.

Always remind yourself that if she is making statements or is behaving in a manner that is out of character, don't take it personally. Know that at some point, the hormones will balance out again, and her irritability and discomfort will diminish. You are both experiencing a huge life change, and for her, there is a huge physical change, too. Both of your emotional needs are great right now. So, your relationship will benefit if you invest time and effort to remain emotionally close to and supportive of her.

And when all of this support is getting too much, be sure to join a support group to gain the support you need or as an expecting couple.

I always remind myself when it feels like I am the one who is putting in all this effort that it's not the time to forget that you're the hen and not the rooster. It's not the time for just a daily cock-a-doodle-doo but to show her you love her through everything you do. Why? Because the more you do, the more you'll feel involved, part of the pregnancy, and closer as a couple.

Show That You're Interested

Growing up on the farm with so many nooks and crannies to tuck away, we became pros at hide and seek. My wife and I get a kick from watching our kids play the game. They are still learning that it's an art to find the balance between being a hiding master but not so good that the other players forget that they're looking for you as they can't find any clues of where you are. Essentially, you need to be somewhat visible to be found.

You'll find yourself in a similar situation now. You need to ensure you're not forgotten; otherwise, you'll be left out of the pregnancy. How can you be sure of this? By showing interest in what's going on.

Be present, physically and mentally, for the relevant conversations. Ask the right questions to start these conversations. Some questions that can be great conversation starters are to discuss practicalities around the nursery, financial management, or how duties and chores will be divided. With our first child, I felt that baby names were something that only became a matter of urgency during the third trimester. While my wife was making baby name lists from day one, it was still taking a while for the whole pregnancy to even feel like reality to me. That is until we chose a name, and I started referring to our unborn son by his name. You can already start to ponder on that, but it's also perfectly acceptable to have a short list and decide together on the name when the baby arrives. Another conversation starter is to ask your partner daily what her concerns are and listen attentively when she shares her vulnerabilities with you.

You can also share how you feel and what you're worried about. But also move onto the positive and share with each other what you're excited or deeply happy about. Discuss the aspects of the pregnancy and journey you both enjoy the most.

Spend quality time together—this often amounts to pampering her since you're choosing to be the best hen for reasons we've already discussed. Don't limit quality time to only a single trimester. Nope! Keep this up for the entire pregnancy; you'll both be grateful you did.

Overcoming Potential Complications

While pregnancy and birth are some of the most natural processes, they can also come with many complications. Even though I don't want us to linger on the possible risks and concerns you may have for too long, the reality remains that you need to prepare yourselves for when things just don't turn out as you've hoped. A miscarriage is a traumatic event in the lives of both parents and while your partner may be in a dark place needing immense support, you shouldn't neglect to get yourself the emotional support you need either.

Miscarriage is a word any expecting parent dreads. The good news is that the percentage of pregnancies that end up in a miscarriage is quite low, ranging in the 10-20% bracket (Miscarriage, n.d.). That said, it's also the case that many miscarriages occur even before your partner realizes she is pregnant. The loss of a baby is called a miscarriage when it occurs before the 20th week of the pregnancy.

If it happens, the most important thing to remember is that nobody is at fault for having a miscarriage. This usually occurs when the fetus isn't developing as it should, and the body automatically rejects any further growth as the baby won't be healthy when born.

Dani's mom experienced multiple miscarriages before becoming pregnant with her, so miscarriage was a topic on our minds from the beginning of our attempts to conceive. When Dani became pregnant for the first time, I felt somewhat in two minds whenever the topic of miscarriage would come up in conversations. It's devastating even when it happens early in pregnancy and something I would rather not dwell on, but I also knew that I had to learn as much as possible to know the risk factors so that we could do everything possible to keep our baby safe.

Some of these factors we could control, while others were entirely beyond our—or any other parent's—control, as you'll see. These are factors like gene or chromosome abnormalities. These abnormalities result when the embryo divides as it grows, and some chromosomes go missing, or extra may be present. It can lead to conditions like a blighted ovum meaning the embryo doesn't form.

Molar pregnancy is another concern and refers to a condition where both chromosomes come from the dad, causing the placenta to grow abnormally while no embryo develops.

Then there is also intrauterine fetal demise, a condition when the embryo forms to a certain point and then stops developing.

Other causes are linked to mom's health, like infections, uncontrolled diabetes, thyroid disease, and other hormonal problems. These were things we could control, and simply by following a healthy lifestyle and being active, Dani could reduce the risk of these factors as I was the supportive hen I had chosen to be. I was supporting her on her health journey all the way.

More things you as the dad can do to reduce the risks you're facing is to ensure you have access to prenatal care, encourage her to reduce her caffeine intake while also cutting back on your own, and support her in taking the necessary multivitamins and prenatal vitamins daily.

But even when you've done everything right, you're still not exempt from the risk of having a miscarriage. Birth is a natural process, and nature takes its own course. We can only do what we can from our side as expecting parents to encourage all to work out well by creating the most optimal environment for the baby to grow.

But while discussing the factors that increase the risk of miscarriage, we also have to discuss the things that won't cause a miscarriage. These are things like exercise or for your partner to continue working. However, it will depend on whether she works in an environment where she is safe and never exposed to harmful chemicals or toxins. And then sexual intercourse —unless your doctor advises you otherwise—won't cause a miscarriage.

One of the most prominent pre-existing conditions that lead to a higher risk of miscarriage is age. After the age of 35, a woman's risk of having a miscarriage is about 20% After 40, this increases to 40%; after 45, the risk of a miscarriage jumps to 80% (Miscarriage, n.d.).

If you've already had miscarriages, you're also more likely to suffer one again.

Alcohol, drugs, and smoking also put your unborn child at risk, as does being highly overweight or even underweight. Cervical problems like weak tissue are another cause for concern, and then certain prenatal tests will also put your baby at risk. Hence, doctors will only do these tests if truly necessary.

Signs of Miscarriage

Let's become familiar with the signs of a miscarriage to ensure your partner gets the best medical care as quickly as possible. Vaginal bleeding or spotting, cramping, pain in the lower back and abdomen, and fluid or tissue passing through the vagina can all be causes for concern. That said, many women have spotting in the first trimester and still have healthy full-term pregnancies. Always promptly contact your physician with any questions or concerns.

What to Do After a Miscarriage

While I wish you the healthiest and happiest pregnancy, I also want you to read the following tips now because if you and your partner suffer the pain and loss of a miscarriage, you're understandably likely to run on autopilot, and it will be good to have this knowledge already. So, remember the following tips, and hopefully, you'll never have to fall back on this information.

- Remember, grief has five stages. Denial, anger, bargaining, depression, and acceptance. These feelings don't always follow this sequence, and each stage can last any amount of time.

- Don't tell your partner that she can always have more kids. This isn't offering any comfort or recognition of the sense of loss she is feeling now. Spend as much time with her as she needs. Maybe she just needs you to sit with her. That can be comforting and helpful too.

- Take care of yourself. You, too, have suffered loss, and you need to go through the process of mourning your unborn child. If you don't feel like talking about it, write it down. Also, consider talking to a professional. It can also help you to get busy. Start a project to honor your unborn child and to get your mind off things. Self-care is vital as that is the only way you'll be able to support your partner effectively without burning yourself out. Remember that both of you need to grieve for as long as necessary.

Ectopic Pregnancy

One more risk factor we haven't touched on yet is ectopic pregnancy. In a normal pregnancy, the fertilized egg would attach itself to the side of the womb. In an ectopic pregnancy, this egg attaches itself to the outside of the main area of the womb, usually in the fallopian tubes. This tube carries the egg from the ovary to the uterus, and if the fertilized egg attaches itself here, it blocks the tube and is called a tubal pregnancy. When this occurs, your partner will still show signs of pregnancy like morning sickness and, of course, miss her period, but this kind of pregnancy can't continue as normal. Early on, there will be vaginal bleeding; if the fertilized egg grows too big, it can cause the tube to rupture, causing a medical emergency. It's excruciatingly painful, and your partner may faint, or her body can go into shock. If she experiences any such symptoms or even shoulder pain—a rather unexpected symptom linked to the concern—it's best to rush her to receive medical care.

Some Secret Dad Tips

It is always good to be prepared; these tips will help you be the most caring and understanding partner you can be.

Tip #1:

Understand her fatigue: During the first trimester, your partner's body is going through immense changes. Her blood pressure increases to accommodate changes in the structure of the placenta. This causes an increase in blood pressure and heart rate. Also, progesterone levels increase during the first trimester, contributing to this fatigue. These changes, coupled with the hard work her body is taking care of to grow a new life, are extremely exhausting, causing her to feel tired all the time.

You can support her by ensuring you both follow a healthy and nutritious diet, remain active, stay hydrated, and get sufficient sleep. Consuming caffeinated drinks won't help. Rather decide to drink water together. And remember to take care of yourself too.

Tip #2:

Be there for her: Whether in the role of protector or comforter, just be there for her throughout the journey. You guys are a team, and team members support each other. Certain smells may make her nauseous. Pregnant women often experience hyperosmia, meaning their sense of smell becomes very strong, often causing nausea and leaving them feeling sick. Clear the home of any smell that may bother her. Prepare her nutrient-dense meals that contain a lot of iron, calcium, and vitamin C to support her body and immune system. When she is sick and vomiting, consuming drinks high in electrolytes will help. Remember that morning sickness can be overwhelming at times, and while having someone who understands by her side will greatly help her, you can also rely on the following tips to make it better for her:

- Avoid preparing excessively spicy food – this can cause acid-reflux.

- She shouldn't take any prenatal supplements or vitamins before eating. These can easily upset the stomach. Taking them right before bed can help lessen the nausea caused by the prenatal.

- Try acupuncture wristbands to reduce nausea.

- Sometimes, essential oils like peppermint can reduce her nausea.

- Have healthy snacks, saltine crackers, dry cereal, or even toast ready to reduce her nausea and relieve her hunger felt after vomiting.

- Herbal ginger supplements can also work, but speak to your doctor first before taking these.

Tip #3:

Pregnancy and sex: You can be intimate during this time, but it's also good to know that your partner's hormonal changes can cause dryness, and blood vessels can rupture more easily than usual. This can lead to vaginal bleeding, but it will be limited, and there is no need for concern as it should clear up in a day or two - if it doesn't, get medical attention.

Intercourse can sometimes be painful due to the dryness your partner may experience, and her breasts and nipples are likely sore or sensitive too. If your partner is experiencing any discomfort, it may be best to seek alternative positions to see if it's better, and if her libido is down, it is also perfectly normal. Don't fret, as it usually picks up again in the next trimester.

Intercourse during the first trimester can be a way to bond and is perfectly safe. That said, if any of the following factors are present, you should wait until you've discussed this with your healthcare provider.

- Vaginal bleeding

- You have experienced preterm labor during a previous pregnancy.

- Amniotic fluid is leaking.

- The placenta covers the cervical opening either entirely or partially.

- The cervix is opening prematurely.

Even if any of the above concerns keep you from having sex with your wife or partner, it's still ok, as there are many more creative ways to be intimate with your partner.

FAQs

Q: Is my partner pregnant?

A: If your partner has missed her period, she is likely pregnant. This can be confirmed with a home pregnancy test. Other early signs are swollen or enlarged breasts, constipation, having to urinate more regularly, fatigue, strange tastes in her mouth, increased vaginal discharge or irritation, and just not feeling like eating or drinking something she used to have.

Q: When do her cravings start?

A: Food cravings are different for everyone. Sometimes it happens as early on as five weeks, and sometimes it's much later on. It can be severe or mild, and it can be for a range of things, even changing during pregnancy. Some women crave fatty foods, while others experience a craving for weird food combinations. You'll earn some high brownie points if you do your best to give her what she craves. But if she starts to crave things like soil, ask your doctor to see if she is missing any key vitamins. Yes, cravings can get a bit crazy!

Q: How much weight should she gain?

A: I advise that under no circumstances do you make any comments about your partner's weight during this time. She is feeling vulnerable and hormonal. A good guideline is that she will likely gain 22-26 lbs. Most of this weight she'll gain after the 20th week. Instead of offering possibly hurtful advice, be a partner in remaining active and eating healthy.

Journal Prompts

It helps to gather your thoughts in writing. I strongly suggest keeping a journal where you can unburden your mental load or ponder specific questions. Following are a couple of prompts to encourage you to put your thoughts and feelings into words.

- How will our lives change after our baby is born?

- What are the possible what-if situations you can already prepare for now?

- What kind of dad do you want to be?

- What are the best memories of your dad you would like to recreate with your child?

- What would you like to teach your child?

Conclusion

*My wife said I should do lunges to stay in shape. That would
be a big step forward.*

Did you let out a guffaw? Are you sharing these awful dad jokes with your
partner? Or are you waiting for that glorious day when you casually drop
a joke on your unsuspecting toddler? In the next chapter, we're exploring
how your little one develops week-by-week throughout the first trimester.

Chapter 4

The 1st Trimester Breakdown

O ne of the best ways to remain involved in the pregnancy is to be sure you know exactly what to expect when it comes to your baby's development, changes taking place in your partner's body, how these changes manifest in the form of symptoms, hormonal changes and what lifestyle changes will best accommodate these changes, the things you need to remember and appointments you need to attend. So, in this chapter, I want to share with you an overview of the first trimester, broken down into 12 weeks. This will also guide you on how to best care for your partner and unborn baby.

Week 1

As the pregnancy date is calculated from the last time your partner has ovulated, there is no baby yet during the first week of pregnancy. Only the most dominant egg cell—the largest single cell in the body— will be released. During this week, the egg cell matures and is ready for ovulation. Conception hasn't occurred yet, but you and your partner can start working towards ensuring a healthy pregnancy by changing your lifestyle to ensure healthy sperm and egg cells. Consider this a team effort to be more active, eat healthy meals, cut down on caffeine, and quit unsavory habits like smoking. During this week, your partner will experience typical menstrual symptoms like cramps, mood changes, headaches, and back pain.

Week 2

Hormonal changes prepare your partner's body for pregnancy to ensure an optimal environment when conception occurs later this week. She is most likely only experiencing menstrual symptoms and an increased sense of smell, while her body temperature can also increase. Her cervical mucus will change consistency and become thin and stretchy to allow the sperm to travel up to the cervix so that conception can occur. Keep up the healthy lifestyle. A helpful tip is to discuss tracking her ovulation cycle if you're actively trying to conceive. Make love often during this time. This is your window!

Week 3

She may not feel any difference, but conception has taken place. The first sign would be that she has missed her period. When taking a pregnancy test, don't be discouraged if it shows negative. It may be that you're just too early. Give it a few days and test again. Other early pregnancy symptoms are fatigue, sore or swollen breasts, nausea or even vomiting, and she has to urinate more frequently. Continue the healthy lifestyle while your partner starts taking a prenatal with folic acid. Once you have a positive pregnancy test, make an appointment with your doctor to confirm it.

Week 4

The embryo (the fetus is first called an embryo during the first eight weeks after conception) is now roughly 0.08 inches (2 mm) long, is the size of a poppy seed, and consists of only two layers of cells. It attaches itself to the uterus lining, where it will grow into your baby. Your doctor will most likely not do an ultrasound yet—these usually only occur after week eight but be prepared for the tiredness to increase, and it's time to step up and help out more around the house to let her rest. She'll still have breast tenderness, while the nausea and vomiting will continue for quite a while. Take care of her by ensuring you have enough fluid for her to drink, preferably with electrolytes to replace what she's lost during vomiting and snacks she feels like eating.

Week 5

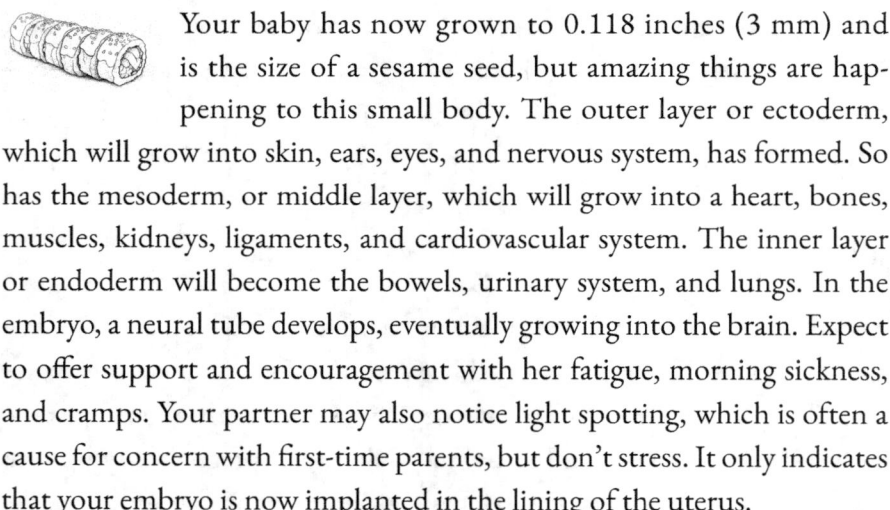 Your baby has now grown to 0.118 inches (3 mm) and is the size of a sesame seed, but amazing things are happening to this small body. The outer layer or ectoderm, which will grow into skin, ears, eyes, and nervous system, has formed. So has the mesoderm, or middle layer, which will grow into a heart, bones, muscles, kidneys, ligaments, and cardiovascular system. The inner layer or endoderm will become the bowels, urinary system, and lungs. In the embryo, a neural tube develops, eventually growing into the brain. Expect to offer support and encouragement with her fatigue, morning sickness, and cramps. Your partner may also notice light spotting, which is often a cause for concern with first-time parents, but don't stress. It only indicates that your embryo is now implanted in the lining of the uterus.

Week 6

 While there will be no baby bump to see yet, know that your partner's uterus is already growing to accommodate your baby. Your baby has grown to 0.25 inches (0.63 cm) and is the size of a lentil. Until about week 12, her uterus will remain within the pelvic bones, so there will be little to no sight of a baby bump. Although you can't see it yet, it's changing shape and looks like an egg pressing down on your partner's bladder. While all the

previous symptoms will persist, she may also start to experience heart-burn, indigestion, and bloating. A healthy diet for this stage includes fresh vegetables, fruits, nuts, grains, and lean animal protein. She should avoid any fish high in mercury, like swordfish and king mackerel, and should stick to omega-3-rich seafood like salmon, light tuna, and shellfish. Staying hydrated and consuming enough fiber will help with constipation. She should also avoid raw fish, eggs, meat, or unpasteurized dairy products due to the higher risks to your baby from foodborne illnesses.

If you have a cat, it's now your responsibility to clean up the litter box, as your partner is at risk of contracting toxoplasmosis, a parasite typically found in cat feces. It's also time to schedule your first antenatal appointment and to start researching the maternity leave policy through her employer. As you'll likely want to spend some time with your new baby, too, you can do the same. Her libido might decrease at this point, so discuss how you want to approach intimacy during this time.

Week 7

Your baby is now about 0.4 inches (1cm), is the size of a blueberry, and your partner's uterus has grown to be about the size of a lemon. While you may want to see a baby bump, this is still not showing. Morning sickness will remain part of your life until about 12-14 weeks (sometimes longer), so be sure to have the necessary snacks and drinks on hand to ensure your partner stays hydrated and have plenty of snack options to choose from when she is peckish. By taking care of your health, you'll encourage your partner to look after herself the best she can too. Maintain a healthy lifestyle and try to remain as active as possible as a couple, but also allow for enough rest when she feels tired. This is the week that genetic testing is usually performed through blood samples. This can be optional but is also recommended for higher-risk pregnancies or families with certain genetic markers. One bonus to this testing is that you can also possibly discover the gender of your baby through testing for the presence or absence of a Y chromosome in the mother's bloodstream!

Week 8

 Your baby showed quite some growth during the past week and is now 0.63 inches (1.6 cm) long from crown to rump and the size of a bean. It will almost double in size next week.

If it's safe, your doctor may consider doing an ultrasound this week, and you'll be able to see that little heart flutter for the first time. Stay fit and healthy, and be as intimate as you would both like. Maybe indulge in a shopping trip for new underwear, as she'll need more supportive bras soon, if not already.

Week 9

 What a journey it has been to this point. Your partner's placenta has now developed completely to supply your baby with sufficient nutrients. Your baby has grown to 0.6-0.7 inches (1.6-1.8 mm) and weighs 0.11 oz (3 g), and is the size of a green olive. What is even more exciting is that its heart has developed four chambers, and you'll be able to hear a heartbeat. Eyelids are becoming more prominent, as well as a nose and ears, and although your partner won't be able to feel them just yet, your baby is already moving its arms and legs. Even its fingers have grown longer, being wider at the ends where fingerprints will form. The same symptoms persist, but she may also develop nasal congestion. This is due to increased mucus production caused by her hormones. Support your partner in her exercise routine and healthy eating. In addition to supportive underwear, she may also feel the need to wear more comfortable clothes.

Week 10

The size of a large strawberry is the best way to describe your baby's size now, as it's approximately 1-1.2 inches (2.54-3 cm) and weighs 0.14 oz (4 g). Calcium will now play an increasingly important role as your baby's bones begin to develop. Other wonders of this time include the development of the spine, still visible through the translucent skin, and teeth forming in their gums. It may be swallowing a lot of amniotic fluid and also peeing, indicating working kidneys. The eyelids are almost completely formed, and their eyes are becoming sensitive to light. Soon, the eyelids will shut completely at the end of the first trimester, as this and other facial features become distinct. You can expect to offer comfort more often as mood swings can feel increasingly difficult for her. Other symptoms remain. Her body will also show more prominent veins as her blood volume increases by roughly 50% during pregnancy. You can start to think about baby names, what you want to do with the nursery, and confirm your due date so that you can start with arrangements. If you haven't announced your pregnancy yet, this will happen soon. Keep up with regular doctor's visits and stay fit and healthy.

Week 11

Your baby is the size of a fig and measures 2 inches (5 cm), and it has fingers and toes while nails start to develop too. Its head is almost half of its body, but this will start to change soon. Your partner's placenta is still expanding and changing to provide your baby with all it needs to grow. By next week, it will completely replace the yolk sac your baby has been utilizing and will soon be the only source of nutrition. Your partner may feel tired more often, which may be the perfect opportunity to cozy up with her to watch a movie. As her belly expands, she may experience pain and discomfort in the joints and ligaments in this area due to a hormone called relaxin, which helps the body loosen and prepare for expansion and birth. It's a good time to visit the dentist since oral health is vital during pregnancy.

During this time, your doctor will advise you of the need for any screening test to ensure your baby is perfectly healthy.

Week 12

By now, your baby's organs, bones, and muscles are in place while its reproductive systems develop. It's about 2 inches (5 cm) long and very similar to a plum while weighing about as much as three grapes or 0.49 oz (14 g). If you haven't made your pregnancy public yet, this secret may be harder to hide from here on out since that baby bump will start showing soon. Increased gas and bloating may leave your partner with stomach cramps, but this is nothing to worry about unless it is accompanied by bleeding. Then, book an appointment with your doctor. Most of the symptoms she has experienced will improve soon as the next 12 weeks are often described as the easiest part of pregnancy - if such a thing exists! Have you and your partner discussed what type of birth would be best? If not, now is a good time. Stretch marks may begin to show. If you don't already do so, remind your partner often of how beautiful she is while helping her rub that soothing lotion on her belly.

Week 13

Your baby is constantly growing and is now roughly 2.8 inches (7 cm) from its crown to the coccyx, or the size of a pea pod, and weighs about 0.89 oz (25 g). The eyes are moving into position, and the upper body is growing rapidly, bringing the head into proportion with the rest of its body. Their reproductive organs are developing; if not already visible, it will soon be possible to confirm their gender. As most of your partner's symptoms have dissipated, including her nausea, she will likely regain her appetite. Often, women experience an increase in libido, which is perfectly fine as you can be intimate as often as you like. Some of the screening tests your doctor may want to do now are for Down's syndrome or other genetic abnormalities. Still, your healthcare professional will advise you on the necessary tests. You and your partner should maintain a healthy lifestyle, and you can continue to look after, care for and support her as you both stay in good health, eat well, and get enough sleep.

First-Time Dads Want to Hear From YOU!

We hope you're enjoying this book and find it entertaining, informative, and valuable as you prepare for your new arrival.

It's your support and feedback that help us in our quest to provide quality resources for expectant fathers like you... Please take 60 seconds to help other new fathers and kindly leave a review on Amazon!

Here's how:

1. **Scan QR code** with your phone's camera

2. **Scroll down & click** "Write a customer review"

Web Link: (*U.S. readers only*)   https://www.amazon.com/review/create-review/?asin=B0CMFGKT79

Embrace your new adventure and enjoy every second because it passes way too fast! From the bottom of our hearts,

THANK YOU for your support!

Part II

Budding Family Books

Chapter 5

Growing Together in the 2nd Trimester

In the pregnancy process, I've realized how much of the burden is on the female partner. She's got a construction zone going on in her belly. —Al Roker

Honestly, your wife does have construction going on in her belly, and, incredibly, you're there to witness every step of the process. So, let's see how you can continue being there.

The Highlights of the 2nd Trimester

The next three months are there for you both to enjoy. Her symptoms will be far less severe, and even though her baby bump will grow, she may still be very comfortable being active and moving. So, what are the highlights to look forward to?

Your Baby Is Moving!

Exciting times when you can feel your baby moving. From 16 weeks on-wards, this movement will become so strong that you can put your hand on your partner's belly and feel your baby move inside.

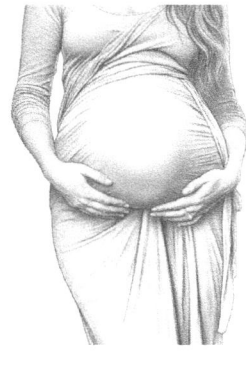

At first, this felt like such a strange thing to me. Placing my hand on Dani's belly and feeling an alien movement gave me the heebie-jeebies. After referring to our child by name and talking directly to him in the womb, this feeling eventually passed. It's simply the most wonderful experience feeling that little boy or girl kick or turn when they hear their dad's sooth-ing voice. It's a beautiful way to start connecting to that miraculous new life. Initially, your partner may experience a feeling like butterflies flying in her stomach. The stronger your baby becomes, the more distinct this movement will become. There is also no specific number of times you should feel your baby move, and your partner will become aware of your baby's cycle over time. Often, babies move more during certain times of the day and sleep in cycles of 20-40 minutes at a time. While you don't have to track every movement, ensuring you feel your baby move every day is best. If neither of you felt your baby move by the time your pregnancy reaches 24 weeks, you should contact your doctor immediately.

Screening, Scans, and Blood Tests

Screens and tests offer a fantastic way to ensure your baby is healthy and continues to grow as expected. However, I must admit that going for these appointments also brings about a bit of anxiety. There is always that little voice in the back of your head saying, what if something is wrong with our baby? It may be challenging to work around one or both work schedules, but try your best to be present for all of these appointments, especially those big ones! You can only imagine how frightening it would be for your partner to receive disheartening information about the pregnancy alone.

Take note of the following tests. It doesn't mean you'll have to go for all these tests, but they are the most common ones scheduled during the second trimester.

13-Week+

Fetal Ultrasound

Now, who doesn't want to see their baby? This is a super exciting visit to your OBGYN as the ultrasound can give you quite a clear image of your baby, and it's usually when your doctor will tell you the gender of your baby. Ultrasound uses sound waves to create 2D images of the placenta and fetus inside the uterus and is a safe way to confirm the baby's size, position, and age. It's often too early to determine gender via ultrasound until around 19-plus weeks. The test holds no risks for your baby or partner, and there is also nothing you need to do to prepare for the test in advance.

You'll simply go in for an appointment, and during the test, the doctor will put gel on your partner's belly and press a hand-held device onto her skin to bring up an image of your baby on the monitor. You'll be able to meet your little one—probably for the first time—while listening to their heartbeat.

15-20-Week Amniocentesis Test

You'll only go for this test if your doctor deems it necessary to perform extra testing to determine Down syndrome, Tay-Sachs disease, or neural tube defects like anencephaly or spina bifida. Other results from such a test are whether fetal lung development is on par and whether your baby has Rh disease.

So, let's quickly explore all these weird words and terms.

- You're most likely familiar with Down syndrome, but in short, it refers to a condition where chromosome abnormalities cause distinct facial features, intellectual disabilities, possible heart defects, and other delays in physical development.

- Tay-Sachs disease isn't a pleasant one to discuss. The disorder is genetic and refers to a state where fatty cells destroy the brain cells. While your baby will live, life expectancy is mostly around four years. The specific gene is present in about 1 out of 300 people and is more common in those of Ashkenazi Jewish descent (Tay-Sachs Disease: Symptoms, Cause, Treatment, 2020).

- Anencephaly is a severe brain defect. Here the baby will be born without parts of the skull and brain, resulting in death if carried full-term.

- Spina bifida refers to a congenital disability where part of the spinal cord is open and not protected by surrounding structures. Babies born with spina bifida can live a full and normal life depending on severity, but it will require several surgeries to enclose the exposed spinal cord.

- Rh disease occurs when the mother's blood type is negative and the baby's is positive. It can lead to a lack of healthy red blood cells distributing oxygen to the rest of the body, putting mom and baby at risk.

Lastly, the procedure can also be used as a treatment for a condition called polyhydramnios. It means there is too much amniotic fluid, and the doctor needs to remove the excess fluid to ensure an optimal environment for your baby to develop.

If this test is done too early on in the pregnancy, it may cause a miscarriage, so your doctor may suggest it only later on. Then there is still this risk for mother and baby, but it's less common. Some risks are cramping, infection, premature labor, leaking of the amniotic fluid, and bleeding.

When it comes to this test, your health provider will explain why they want to have it done, but the choice remains yours whether you wish to proceed with it.

It's a minimally intrusive procedure. The medical expert will clean a small area on your partner's belly with antiseptic before applying gel for the ultrasound to monitor your baby during the procedure. Next, your doctor will insert a thin but hollow needle through her abdomen into the uterus to draw a sample of amniotic fluid. Once this is done, they will monitor the movement and heartbeat of your baby to ensure they're fine. This fluid gets sent to a lab where they'll analyze the sample to check for abnormalities. Within a week or two, you'll have the results.

The entire process is 99% accurate and is done within 30 minutes, during which your partner will only experience discomfort or a small amount of pain. She must relax and take things slow for the rest of the day.

It's similar to DNA screening when doctors examine the DNA of the placenta released into your partner's blood. Doctors can screen for Down syndrome, Edwards syndrome, and other concerns through this kind of testing.

15–22-Week Genetic Screening

This test determines if your baby has any genetic disorders. Parents or couples planning on becoming parents can have a blood test done to determine whether they're carriers of genetic disorders. Medical experts also look at the development of the heart, facial features, and abdomen to determine any abnormalities. The first screening may occur during the first trimester and another during the second trimester if there is cause for concern.

18-21-Week Anomaly Scan

This detailed ultrasound is available to all, but you can still decline. We never declined because it's also the scan where you can learn the baby's gender – and we weren't about to wait until birth! The predominant reason for this scan, though — which doesn't put the mother or baby at risk — is to check for rare but still possible developmental conditions in your baby.

During the scan, the doctor will observe and take precise measurements of the growth of your baby's abdomen, heart, spinal cord, face, kidneys, bones, and brain.

Helping Your Partner in the 2nd Trimester

As a dad of three, this is my advice to you as I want you and your partner to enjoy this time of the pregnancy.

Help your partner as much as possible in and around the house. I've said it before and will probably say it again, do things before you're asked. She'll appreciate your help so much more if she doesn't even have to ask for it. Also, be sure that you carry all the heavy things so that she doesn't risk her body while it's your baby's construction site.

Help her stay relaxed. I firmly believe that the less stress your partner experiences during her pregnancy, the more relaxed your baby will be when born. If you've been attending antenatal classes, you can use the techniques you've learned here to alleviate the stress.

It is also time to discuss your paternity leave with your employer. Research your employer's paternity leave policy, what it entails, and how you should request it. Some of the benefits of paternity leave are pretty obvious, but let's just recap. This time with your partner and baby offers a fantastic opportunity to establish your role as a parent who is actively involved in your child's life. As you'll be more present for your partner, it also improves your relationship and the bond that exists between the two of you playing on the same team.

Another way to care for your partner is by considering her need for intimacy. It's usual for her libido to increase greatly during the second trimester. So, assuming you aren't at high risk and haven't been told to hold off by your doctor, keep that connection alive and have some fun!

6 Conversations to Have With Your Partner

While some of these conversations may only become relevant after birth, it's good to have them now before your baby is born and your partner is feeling hopefully better as the symptoms of the first trimester are over and before she isn't as uncomfortable as during the third trimester.

The following six conversations are a must-have during this time, especially when your first baby is on the way.

#1 Caring for Your Relationship

Put plans in place to prioritize your relationship after your baby is born. What are the things you're willing to commit to now to ensure that once you take your baby home, you two will still make time for each other and intimacy?

#2 Social Media Exposure

You and your partner should agree on how much you'll share of your pregnancy and your baby's life after birth. Some parents are very strict about sharing photos and information about their children on their social media platforms, while others love sharing images of their little ones. The choice is yours, and the only person you need to agree with is your partner.

#3 Your Wishes During Delivery

You've also been dreaming about the day when your baby is born and have certain ideas, hopes, and dreams of what you imagine would happen in the delivery room. Yet, your partner will only know and accommodate your wishes if you express them to her. It's why it's so vital to have an open line of communication in place. By talking about it, you can easily align your intentions and dreams for the day and be sure to have the experience you both want.

#4 How Much Access to Give Visitors and In-Laws

What will you do if many people rush to meet your new baby? Sure, this is an exciting moment, but it can also be exhausting, and you may not feel like dealing with so many people. Determine in advance what boundaries you'll set and how you will maintain these boundaries when challenged. After all, you want to treat your family and friends who deeply care about you with kindness, but you can also protect your new family. Just remember that you may decide on something now and then change your mind later on, which is okay too.

#5 Me-Time

Draft a plan in advance that will guide you to become the parents and partners possible. Detail how and when you will both relax and recharge. You can discuss your schedule now to ensure you both have ample moments for a time-out to prevent parental burnout.

#6 Returning to Work

It's a good time to discuss how and when one or both of you will be returning to work. Will you be alternating? Utilizing a sitter while you both go back to keep your careers alive? Or will one of you be a stay-at-home parent for now?

Antenatal Classes

As a first-time dad-to-be, I didn't know anything about antenatal classes and didn't understand why we needed to go. While I know that this is often a paid service, our hospital offered it for free—a nice touch, but it also made me doubt whether it would be worth our time—but Dani had her mind set on going. While I might not have been committed to antenatal classes, I was committed to supporting my wife in every possible way. Well, that is history, and today I know that antenatal classes are probably even more important for you to attend than for your partner. It's a place where you can connect with other couples, especially dads, who are in the same situation as you.

In these classes, you get prepared for birth and learn to efficiently identify the signs of labor so that you can get to the hospital on time. You learn about the stages of labor, how to help your partner relax with breathing techniques, and support her through the birthing process. But you'll also learn more about breastfeeding and what that entails, how to look after your baby during those very early days, and what to expect behavior-wise from your newborn. These classes made me feel more involved in the pregnancy, and without the knowledge we've gained here, I can only imagine that we would've been far more stressed out during those first couple of days—perhaps even weeks–after coming home from the hospital. It empowered us to understand that our baby's behavior was perfectly normal.

Depending on where you stay, you may be able to find a selection of different types of antenatal classes in your area. For example, there are classes for early pregnancy and for preparation for breastfeeding classes. Lamaze classes focus primarily on breathing techniques and positions to help your partner feel prepared for the birthing experience and manage her pain more effectively.

Hypnobirthing is also a wonderful option for pain management during labor and entails several breathing, meditation, and visualization techniques. By getting familiar with these techniques, you can support your partner during labor, helping her manage her stress hormone levels, reduce pain, and even shorten the process.

Active birth classes explore birthing positions and techniques, while calm birth classes share a deeper insight into the process. Then there are also aqua antenatal classes and classes incorporating yoga and pilates. You can even find classes for parents expecting more than one baby or who are choosing to give birth by cesarean. And yes, some of these classes are even available online. While this kind of setup offers an entirely different sense of community, you can still learn a lot and have the same sense of bond-building as when attending a class in person.

The easiest way to find antenatal classes near you is to ask your doctor or midwife for recommendations.

Overcoming Complications

Mom and baby are a duo pack. It means that during pregnancy and birth, there are a range of complications that can impact the mom or baby individually or have an impact on both. While these concerns physically impact their health, they will also impact your life as a dad. While you may not experience the same physical bond as your partner, you are still very much a part of the emotional bond that exists already with your unborn child.

Knowing what you need to be prepared for is better than being caught off-guard. We have already explored some of the many tests and screening processes that you may have to do, but let's see what complications doctors can detect.

1st Trimester Screening

During weeks 11-13 of your first trimester, your doctor will be doing tests to look for congenital issues using the maternal blood test and ultrasound to diagnose chromosomal disorders like Down syndrome. The blood test can detect if protein levels are higher or lower than expected, while the ultrasound can detect a build-up of fluid in your baby's neck, which can indicate a heart defect or chromosomal disorder.

2nd Trimester Screening

These screening processes take place between weeks 10 and 15, and there are predominantly three types of tests to keep in mind.

A fetal echocardiogram explores the sound waves of your baby's heartbeat and provides a clear image of the heart to determine if there are any abnormalities or defects to consider. However, if the doctor notices any abnormalities in your baby's heart, they'll likely do more tests to look for congruent health concerns.

Doctors use a maternal serum screen which is essentially another blood test to test for protein abnormalities in your partner's blood to determine concerns like neural tube defects and also again for Down syndrome.

They may do another fetal echocardiogram to monitor the development of your baby's heart.

Lastly, an anomaly ultrasound is a specific type of ultrasound offering a very clear image of your baby to check for any other abnormalities. This ultrasound is usually done between weeks 18 and 20.

Diagnostic Tests

First of all, I want to say most of these tests are only relevant when you're having a high-risk pregnancy and there is a cause for concern. High-risk pregnancies would be when your partner is older than 35, suffer from chronic diseases like lupus, or had a previous pregnancy where there was a birth defect.

Under the umbrella term of diagnostic tests, you'll find a high-resolution ultrasound, giving clear images of the details of your baby's appearance to see if there are any abnormalities. This ultrasound should be done between 18 and 20 weeks.

A chorionic villus sampling or CVS requires that doctors take a small sample of the placenta or the chorionic villus. Through this test, they can detect any genetic or chromosomal disorders in your baby. Usually, this test will only be done now when there are abnormal results during the first trimester or if your partner is a high-risk mom.

During amniocentesis, the doctor will draw a small sample of the amniotic fluid to test your baby's protein levels. Any abnormalities in this regard can indicate issues like cystic fibrosis, Tay-Sachs disease, Down syndrome, or other genetic problems. This test should be done between 15 and 18 weeks.

Abnormalities Determined After Birth

The reality is that even with all these tests now possible due to advances in modern medicine, there are still certain birth defects that can only be detected once your baby is born. If the doctors determine any such defect, they'll explore your family's health history to determine if there are any hereditary concerns, and if they're not able to find what they need to know, your doctor will refer you to a specialist for a more accurate diagnosis.

This is never the favorable part of pregnancy, and I hate being the bearer of news that might leave you feeling stressed about your unborn baby, but there are several silver linings around this dark cloud. The weightiest one being the number of healthy babies born by far outshines the number of those born with complications. Another silver line is that with modern medicine, many babies grow up to live healthy and happy lives when they receive the correct treatment.

A defect can also go undetected for the longest time. It's vital to have enough information on the matter—not to drive yourself crazy with concern—but to be informed and make smart choices when you notice anything that seems odd during any stage of your child's life.

So, your priority as a parent in this regard is to educate yourself on the matter to identify the signs and symptoms early on. The second is identifying your support network to carry you through difficult times.

Complications Impacting Your Partner's Health

Before going any further, remember I'm sharing the experience, knowledge, and understanding I've gained going through the pregnancy and birth processes with my wife. Although Dani and I have had three children, we are NOT doctors and aren't qualified to give medical advice. If at any point you are concerned about your partner's health, don't delay contacting your physician. Only a qualified medical expert can provide proper advice and guidance after making a diagnosis.

That said, let's move on to some of the possible health concerns your partner may be facing.

Gestational Hypertension

Maybe your partner hasn't suffered from hypertension before pregnancy, and now she does. This condition is called gestational hypertension, and it causes the arteries transporting blood from the heart to the organs to narrow, increasing the pressure in the arteries and making it challenging for sufficient blood supply to reach the placenta. This can result in the placenta not receiving enough nutrients or oxygen to support your baby. Preterm labor and preeclampsia are complications that can stem from this issue.

Preeclampsia is a condition that only becomes relevant during the second trimester and will pass after birth. Does your partner suffer symptoms like a constant headache, sudden weight gain except for her natural pregnancy gain, nausea and vomiting after morning sickness was over, pain in her belly or stomach area, edema (swelling due to fluid buildup in tissues), only being able to produce small amounts of urine, or have blurry or double vision? Then it might be better to have her checked out, as preeclampsia can risk your partner's and baby's lives. Eclampsia occurs when untreated preeclampsia progresses to involve the central nervous system, leading to seizures, coma, or possibly death. It's a serious but rare condition that can develop late in pregnancy, during labor, or in the early postpartum stage. The only cure for eclampsia is the delivery of the baby. Other issues that stem from untreated gestational hypertension are poor fetal growth, stillbirth, seizures, or the placenta detaching from the uterus too early.

Gestational Diabetes

Gestational diabetes doesn't show many symptoms except for more frequent urination. It's another health concern that may not have been previously present, only to show up during pregnancy. This condition can lead to your baby having breathing difficulty when born, carrying excess birth weight, suffering from obesity or type 2 diabetes later in life, stillbirths, and premature births. It puts your partner's health at risk as it can cause hypertension and preeclampsia, future diabetes, and makes it more likely that she'll need a C-section.

Gestational diabetes is a health concern that is usually preventable with a healthy diet and remaining active. It's also less likely to become a problem if your partner was already of a healthy weight when you got pregnant or if she takes care not to put on more weight than necessary.

Iron-Deficiency Anemia

Extreme fatigue, pale skin, brittle nails, chest pains, weakness, inflammation or soreness of her tongue, headaches, dizziness, unusual cravings for things like soil or chalk, shortness of breath, and a poor appetite are all symptoms of iron-deficiency anemia. If you are concerned that your partner may be suffering from any of these ailments, it is best to visit your physician, who may prescribe her a pregnancy-safe iron supplement. With her nausea and eating habits changing, consuming enough iron without needing supplemental aid is sometimes difficult.

As I've already mentioned, your partner's body is a construction site of new life, and her iron stores need to be sufficient to supply the needs of her body and the needs of your ever-growing baby.

Symphysis Pubis Dysfunction

Between the left and right pelvic bones is a joint tied together with ligaments, allowing for movement. When these ligaments loosen during pregnancy to prepare the body for birth, it can cause pain, a condition called symphysis pubis dysfunction (SPD). The condition can cause your partner to feel mild pain and discomfort, which can sometimes evolve, causing sharp shooting pains in her back, groin, and lower abdomen. It can be worse when she bends forward or walks, making it harder to climb stairs, get in or out of a car, get onto the bed, or raise a leg. It can also cause pain and difficulty when using the toilet, and she may also be tired often. She may even hear a clicking sound from the shifting bones and loose ligaments coming from her abdomen that can be enough to affect her mood too.

You can be of great support to help her deal with this pain and discomfort. Giving her an ice pack for the pelvic area or sacrificing those extra pillows on the bed to sleep with between her knees can aid in some relief. Comfortable shoes and a pregnancy belt or support band can ease discomfort.

Amniotic Fluid Complications or Hydramnios

Amniotic fluid is vital to sustaining your baby's health, but it must be present in the right quantities.

Too much fluid can result in preterm labor as it places much pressure on your partner's uterus and diaphragm, leading to difficulty breathing. This concern is mainly caused by incompatible blood types, birth defects, when your partner suffers from uncontrolled gestational diabetes, or you're expecting multiple babies. Too little fluid can result in stillbirth, slowed growth, or congenital disabilities.

A common symptom includes discomfort in the abdomen due to rapid growth of the uterus and uterine contractions. Other symptoms can present similarly to those of other health concerns. So, the best way to support your partner is to validate the discomfort she may be experiencing and support her in contacting the doctor whenever she doesn't feel well. This concern can usually be detected with an ultrasound, and several treatment options exist to resolve this issue.

Again, these are all scary subjects, but my motto is preparation over panic. When you're informed, it's much easier to work as a team, remain unruffled, and face unforeseen circumstances head-on.

Secret Dad Tips

Tip #4:

Prepare and stock up on freezer meals: Do this before your baby's due date. There aren't many things that can turn the usual harmony of your home into chaos, like the arrival of your newborn baby. So, do your best to prepare those things you can in advance. Getting stocked up on food that is easy to defrost and having a decent meal with your partner while you're both exhausted will be a saving grace you'll both be grateful for, not to mention how helpful a quick bite can be when there is no time to sit down to eat.

Dos

Make enough meals that consist of easy bites that you can hold in one hand while your baby is in the other. Listen, there may come times that you'll get so hungry, you feel like gnawing on your fingers, but there is no time to sit down and have a meal. Then these bites are just what you need as you run around making bottles, putting in an-other load of laundry, or taking care of yet another task that screams for your urgent attention. It also makes it easier for others to feed you when both hands are occupied, but you still need to eat.

Don'ts

Don't make too many meals that require you to sit down and eat with a fork and a knife. There may not always just not be time to do this.

Don't forget that there are several meals during the day—you may need a bite for breakfast too. People may bring you lasagne or a casserole when you bring your baby home, but nobody ever brings you anything for breakfast. If you like having fruit for breakfast, it may be easy, but also consider things like granola bars or easy refrigerated overnight oats.

Tip #5:

Take a babymoon: Maybe you never had the time or the money to go on a honeymoon, or perhaps you did. Either way, now is a great time to book a quick escape with your partner. If she and your baby are in good health, then the second trimester is a great part of the pregnancy to do this. Having a baby will make it hard to get away for the first couple of years after birth, so you don't know when you'll have a chance again. It's a perfect time to spend as a couple before becoming parents.

If you're going to travel abroad, consider things like whether she will still be able to fly. (This is usually only a concern in the third trimester). Consider taking a direct flight to make travel easier for her. Don't overbook your break and focus on spending quality time together rather than doing many things or immersing yourself in sightseeing. As your family grows, so do your family's financial needs, so remain moneywise and don't overspend the babymoon budget.

Tip #6:

Help with or plan the baby shower: Typically, a friend or family member will be in charge of the baby shower, but there are still many ways you can help the host. You may be able to share the needed contact details for the guest list or make food for the party. You'll also be able to tell her the essentials you still need for your baby, as this knowledge makes it much easier to plan a baby registry. A baby registry is helpful to ensure you get the things you still need for your baby. A newer shower custom is to include men and women, especially for those with a large pool of friends or family. Dani played host to one of her her sister's showers. They called a BaBy-Q that included all our family, men and women, and we had a great relaxing time while barbecuing! Ask what the mom-to-be envisions for the shower, and make it happen!

FAQs

Q: Do we buy a crib or bassinet for the nursery?

A: When your nursery is very small, a bassinet—which is smaller in size, may be a better purchase as it requires less space, and then there is also the added benefit that it's relatively mobile. However, if you only want to make this purchase once and want it to last long enough until your baby can sleep in a bed, a crib would be the better investment, as babies can outgrow a bassinet quite quickly. We preferred having the baby sleep in a bassinet in our room for the first couple of months. When the baby started sleeping longer stretches at night, we put them in their own room in a crib.

Q: What type of breast pump is the best?

A: There is no better or worse breast pump, and it all boils down to what would best suit your needs and what makes your partner feel comfortable. There are two kinds of pumps: manual and electric. Manual breast pumps are cheaper, smaller, simpler to use, lightweight, and quieter if pumping needs to happen where your baby is sleeping. An electric pump is much quicker and far less labor-intensive but can be noisy and expensive.

Q: Which types of baby bottles should we buy?

A: As with breast pumps, the best investment to make is one that suits your unique needs.

- Standard bottles are readily available and affordable.

- Heat-sensitive bottles are great as they change color when the milk is too hot.

- Wide-neck bottles may be bulky but clean easily.

- Anti-colic bottles keep your baby from taking in air while drinking.

- Glass bottles are great for the environment but will break easily.

- Self-sterilizing bottles don't require much cleaning except for putting them in the microwave.

Checklist

Have you felt your baby moving yet? Make a point of doing so daily to start forming a bond with your little one. This is also a great way to spend precious time with your partner.

- Book all your screening and test appointments

- Decide how to keep the romance alive after your baby is born.

- Agree on your social media policy. How much will you be sharing about your baby?

- Set your boundaries regarding hospital visits after your baby's birth.

- How will you communicate these boundaries and enforce them?

- Book antenatal classes and attend.

- Start finding recipes to prepare in advance.

- Are you going to spoil yourself and your partner with a baby-moon? Determine what your budget is and book it.

- Who is planning the baby shower? Check in and see how you can assist. Perhaps you can set up the baby registry.

Conclusion

Why do fathers take an extra pair of socks when they go golfing? In case they get a hole-in-one!

Again, share a chuckle with your partner because her hormones are still on a rollercoaster during the second trimester. However, the changes are bringing you closer to the third trimester, where you'll discover how to become an expert on all things pregnancy and delivery.

Chapter 6

The Second Trimester Breakdown

K nowledge remains power. By educating yourself on how your baby is developing, how this growth impacts your partner's body, and how she feels, you're better equipped to offer the support your partner needs. It's also how you'll remain involved, establishing yourself as an involved parent from before your baby is born. It's good for you, your partner, and your relationship to be involved to this extent. So, let's overview weekly development during the second trimester.

Week 14

 Your baby has now grown to the same size as a peach and is 3.1 - 3.9 inches (8 - 10 cm) long, weighs about 0.8 - 1.2 oz (25 - 35 g), and can turn its head, move limbs, and will even suck its finger. They can reach out and grasp things like the umbilical cord. Their eyebrows and lashes are starting to grow, and as their features develop, their facial muscles are also working better now. As their joints develop, they can move more with greater coordination. Your baby's body is covered with lanugo. Lanugo is thin hair that will be almost completely gone by birth. While its respiratory system is already busy developing, it still relies on the placenta to breathe.

Your partner's energy levels will typically improve by now, and she'll have a healthier appetite. She may start to develop varicose veins as the pressure on her belly increases. Another point to consider during this time is that couvade syndrome might appear. It's also called sympathetic pregnancy, affecting about 50% of all fathers. This includes physical responses to their partner's pregnancy, including weight gain, backache, food cravings, and mood swings. So, if you find yourself with cravings or put off by what used to be your favorite meal, that's all it is. If you don't have these experiences, you're also perfectly fine.

Week 15

 From crown to rump, your baby is about 4 inches (10 cm) long and the size of an apple. It weighs roughly 0.15 lbs (70 g). The vital organs are formed and busy developing while their bones become harder. Your baby is also practicing breathing and pulling amniotic fluid through the nose. Other reflexes they are practicing include sucking and swallowing. Your partner's uterus has now developed to the point where it's pointing upwards, and suddenly, she might look much more pregnant than before. It's also around this time that the Linea nigra appears. This is a dark line that runs from the belly button to the pelvis. Don't be worried about this line; it disappears gradually after birth.

As your baby grows stronger, your partner will gain more quickly. She may experience heartburn more often and have a stuffy nose due to her hormones that increase circulation to all mucus membranes. This can even result in nose bleeds occasionally, while her gums may be swollen or sore too. It's important to continue a healthy lifestyle that includes enough activity. She must also remember her regular dental visits and be sure to remind her of taking her calcium supplements. This is a great time to really start to brainstorm on possible baby names if you haven't decided on any yet. Soon, you'll know the gender of your baby (if you've decided to do so) and can start naming it.

Week 16

The size of an avocado best resembles your baby's body now as it's about 4.7 inches (12 cm) long and weighs 3.5 oz (100 g). The great news is that its heart is starting to pump blood, and its movements become more purposeful and directed. Your baby can also hear your voice, making it a great time to talk to it, as it's known that babies can remember the sounds they hear in their mother's belly. Have you seen signs of pregnancy brain in your partner yet? This isn't just a myth. Due to all the changes taking place in her body, the rate of brain cell renewal slows down, resulting in brain fog. It can be very frustrating to her, so have patience. A good change is that the state of her hair and nails will improve due to the additional estrogen and androgen hormones that leave her with a healthy glow.

It's time to consider how you'll outfit the nursery, what you need to purchase, and where to find the best prices. Spend quality time together on another shopping trip if she doesn't already have well-fitting maternity clothes.

Week 17

Your baby is responding to sound! It's the size of a big potato, is 5.1 inches (13 cm) long, and looks more like a little human. The eyelids are now fully developed, and its eyes are mostly closed. Your partner has her pregnancy glow. There is more blood circulation to her vital organs, and coupled with the increased hormones, she'll look healthy and radiant. Compliment her on her looks as she might feel uncomfortable in her body as her baby bump rapidly increases. It might become more challenging for her to find a comfortable sleeping position. She might also be dealing with headaches, bleeding nose or gums, indigestion, and bloating. If she is struggling with a swollen or stuffy nose, a humidifier in the bedroom can help her breathe and improve her snoring so that you both can get a good rest at night.

Week 18

Your baby can make a fist, and it's now 5.5 inches (14 cm) long, weighs about 7.1 oz (200 g), and is the size of a bell pepper. You can start to feel these controlled punches if you put your hand on your partner's belly. The movement will be more prominent now that your baby has grown so much bigger. Your partner may feel weird in her body as her belly and breasts are much larger than what she is used to. Some women complain that they're feeling clumsy, and there is no better time than right now to tell your partner how amazing she looks and boost her confidence with compliments.

If she is experiencing any spotting or unusual vaginal discharge, pain or burning when urinating, vomiting, pain below her ribs, or swelling of her face, hands, feet, or ankles, it's always best to visit the doctor. Make self-care a priority in your home for you and her. As her belly gets bigger, she may only be able to eat small meals without discomfort. Prepare a couple of snacks or healthy treats for her to grab whenever necessary.

Week 19

Your baby is the size of a mango as it's 6 inches (15.3 cm) long and weighs about 8.5 oz (240 g). At this point, it's typically positioned with its feet towards the bottom of the uterus and its head upwards. Its reproductive systems have developed quite a bit by now, meaning if it's a girl, her uterus and vagina are in place, and if it's a boy, his genitalia will also already be there. It only needs to develop a little more. Your partner may be hungry more often, have abdominal cramps as your baby is growing so rapidly inside of her, and it's quite common now to see her jump around with a cramp in her leg. Your duty? To rub these out, feed her when she is hungry, and listen to her whenever she feels frustrated with her body that looks so much different than what she is used to or with her brain fog hampering her productivity. Encourage her to take time out for self-care, and you should do the same. Remember your doctor's appointments, and be sure to be there as much as possible.

Week 20

 Forgetfulness, shortness of breath, indigestion, heartburn, constipation, increased vaginal discharge, and lower back pain are only some of the symptoms your partner may have as your baby has now grown to be the size of a grapefruit. Yes, your baby is now 6.3 inches (16 cm) long from the head to the coccyx and 9.8 inches (25 cm) from head to toe and weighs about 10.6 oz (0.3 kg). Rubbing her feet throughout the day will reduce cramping and swelling in her legs, while a belly band will support her belly. Your baby can now distinguish between sounds and may already have a sleep pattern. They can also get hiccups now, causing a string of flurry movements in your partner's uterus. Your baby's skin is gradually becoming less translucent, too, as skin cells are developing. Even though she has a much larger belly bump, you can still make love if you're both in the mood to do so. Finding new and more comfortable positions will be fun and bring you closer together. Have you discussed paternity leave with your employer yet? If not, don't delay for much longer.

Week 21

From crown to heel, your baby is now the length of a banana, is 10.5 inches (26.6 cm) long, and weighs about 14.1 oz (400 g). As a baby's taste buds develop, it's beginning to taste the different foods your partner is eating that end up in the amniotic fluid. The cartilage in the joints is growing thicker and stronger, making movements more prominent. Some symptoms your partner may experience are acne, back pain, flatulence, urinary tract infections, and Braxton Hicks contractions, often confused for early labor, leaving parents distressed, but it is only the body preparing itself for labor. Sounds like fun, right? Be there for your partner physically and emotionally, as she may not always admit it, but this is a time of high vulnerability, and I am sure you want her to feel secure and protected with you by her side.

Week 22

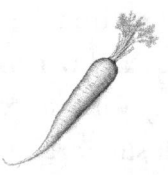

Your baby doesn't have a lot of fatty tissue yet, so it looks tall and thin and is the size of a carrot. It's 11 inches (28 cm) long and weighs about 1 pound (450 g). Its liver is kicking in and producing enzymes while breaking down bilirubin, a byproduct when red blood cells are broken down. Its sensory system is developing, and another amazing development is that if you're having a girl, her egg cells are already formed. That means that the cells that will bring you grandchildren are already developed. Interesting, right? It's little bits of information like this that make pregnancy so exciting and that help you feel involved as a dad. If you don't know the gender of your baby yet, you'll surely soon know.

Your partner is likely feeling quite uncomfortable. I mean, the cramps, nausea, Braxton Hicks contractions, varicose veins, constipation, hemorrhoids, flatulence, and abdominal pain, are enough to remind us why we're just the hen, and she is the one making the biggest sacrifice for our family. Are you supporting her emotionally? Are you thinking about other ways to be intimate? Sure, you can still have sex and appreciate her increased libido, but with all that is going on in her body, she might not feel so sexy anymore. Be creative and also find ways to stay intimate beyond intercourse.

Week 23

By now, your baby's organs, necessary for survival outside of the womb, have developed, and it has grown to the size of a zucchini. It's 11.2 inches (28.5 cm) long and weighs 1.1 pounds (478 g). The bones in its ears have developed, and he or she can respond even better to loud sounds or music. Your partner may start to notice stretch marks on her belly and hips. She'll still experience the same symptoms, and this will likely be the case until birth. Sleeping may become harder for her, so spoil her with a full-body pillow that supports her to get well-deserved rest. It's time to work on your birthing plan and be sure that you're getting your hospital bag packed and ready to grab. How far along is your nursery? What more do you need to buy until it's ready for your baby?

Week 24

At the size of an eggplant which is 11.5 inches (29 cm) long and weighs about 1.3 lbs (580 g), your baby may be kicking much harder and more consistently. All body parts have been developed and will be growing stronger and more defined, while mom's bump will also be growing. Now is also the time to reflect on possible symptoms of some of the complications we've discussed in previous chapters and to book appointments for the relevant screenings. Compile lists of concerns you may have and take them along on your doctor's visits to get the answers you need to put your mind at ease. You can also start to play soothing music or sing to your baby. This may feel a little silly, but once they're born, these will be the songs that will be the most effective in easing crying. PS. You can thank me later for this bit of insight.

Week 25

Your baby is about the size of an ear of corn, weighing roughly 1.7 lbs (785 g), and is 13.1 inches (33.6 cm) long. It's now quite a mover in your partner's belly. Its nose and nostrils are functioning, and it's breathing in amniotic fluid supporting lung development. However, their lungs aren't quite ready to oxygenate blood, and they need to stay put in there for a few weeks longer. Another symptom that may also show up is your partner's restless legs. This can be improved by taking a supplement containing vitamin B12, iron, folate, and magnesium. Just be sure to check this with your doctor before she takes any meds—even supplements. Dani experienced tear-inducing leg cramps that would wake her up from a dead sleep. Rubbing her legs and utilizing a heating pad helped significantly. Stay by your partner's side, and if you're planning a babymoon—now is the time to do so.

Week 26

With a pumping heart and working blood vessels, your baby is growing fast and is about the size of a large beetroot, leaves, and all. Yep! Your baby is 14 inches long (35.6 cm) and weighs 2 lbs (907 g). The umbilical cord has also grown thicker to accommodate an increased need for nutrients, and following a healthy and nutritional diet is just as important as ever. Your partner is still gaining weight, so be kind and considerate of how she may feel about her body right now. You may notice your baby sticking out its tongue or waving its hands when going for an ultrasound. The exciting news is that your doctor will also be able to confirm the gender of your baby accurately! Now, you can finalize the last accessories in the nursery.

Week 27

Your baby is developing rapidly, and finer details like its retinae are developing fast. It has more definite sleep and awake patterns. It's 14.4 inches (36.6 cm) long, weighs 2.1 lbs (950 g), and is roughly the size of a cauliflower. Your partner may notice that your baby responds differently when exposed to various sensations, like being more active when drinking very hot or cold beverages. Her body is going into the final stretch of pregnancy, and she must be getting enough rest. When on meal duty, steer clear of the hot and spicy stuff. While it's perfectly safe for her to eat that chicken with creamy jalapeno sauce, it may cause unnecessary heartburn and indigestion due to a slower-running digestive tract. It's safe to have intercourse throughout the entire pregnancy unless instructed otherwise by your doctor due to a high-risk pregnancy. Continue to remain intimate and emotionally close as parents-to-be.

Part III

Budding Family Books

Chapter 7

Preparing for the 3rd Trimester

Becoming a father is easy enough, but being one is very rough.
—Wilhelm Busch

It's a hard-hitting quote with oodles of truth. However, the time is coming closer for you to be a father. So, let's ensure you're mentally ready and prepared for anything. I'm sure that the arrival of the third trimester felt like it happened way faster than it felt for your partner. By now, her baby bump is quite large, and she is most likely very uncomfortable. Both her body and mind have had enough of the hormone overload, and she may be in greater anticipation for the birth of your baby than you. That said, it's even more important for you to give her the physical and emotional support she needs now while also taking care of yourself to ensure you, too, are ready for your baby's arrival.

Interesting Facts and Changes

So, what is happening inside and out of the rapidly growing baby bump? A lot, but for starters, there is definitely a lot of movement. As long as there is regular movement, all is good inside, and you can rest assured that your baby is growing stronger. Consider these movements as your baby's way of communicating, letting you know all is well and good inside the womb.

Each baby moves differently, and there are no set guidelines on what you should be looking for, but by now, your partner is used to the movement of your baby. If there is a sudden change in movement or your partner can't feel the baby moving for a while, it's best to see your doctor without delay. It may be that your baby is in distress or not feeling as well. Expect movements to increase the closer you get to the due date.

The movements of your baby will also be more directed and focused as certain reflexes develop. By now, the suck reflex shows up around week 32 and continues to improve until around week 36, and during this time, they may be sucking on their fingers or hands. Every ultrasound image that we had during the pregnancy of our second child depicted her sucking her thumb. She was a thumb sucker through toddlerhood. It's amazing how their habits are already developing within the womb.

While your baby won't be born for another 2-3 weeks, a pregnancy is considered full-term at 37 weeks. By now, everything is fully developed, and your baby is ready to be born, but it will still hang in there for a while to grow stronger in the safety and comfort of mum's belly—at least for the baby.

If both partners feel in the mood for lovemaking, know that sex during the third trimester is entirely possible and safe. There may just be some interesting changes in her body, like leaky breasts or tinges of blood after sex. While her breasts may leak all on their own, it's usually caused by sexual stimulation. This fluid is called colostrum - the rich pre-milk your baby will need once born. Colostrum contains fats, carbohydrates, white blood cells, protein, and antibodies.

Noticing a little bit of spotting is also perfectly fine. Nobody got hurt, and the spotting is only the result of the uterus being soft and enlarged.

Intercourse has been said to induce labor. This is only partially true. Instead, the oxytocin and prostaglandins released during sex along with the contractions of the uterus during orgasm, don't initiate labor but can definitely aid the processes already in play. Whether you realize it or not, during these last few weeks, her body is heavily preparing for labor. Another benefit of sex during the third trimester is that many women sleep better after intercourse.

Helping Your Partner in the 3rd Trimester

Whether you typically have a division of chores or work together on all housework, now is as good a time as any to figure it all out. There are a lot of tasks you can relieve from your partner. Not just taking care of the heavy lifting but taking on more than your typical responsibilities. Give her time to rest her swollen ankles by sitting up high with her feet. Pregnancy is a well-designed prep course to prepare you both to share the mental (and physical when it comes to housework) load of parenthood.

Remember that even simple movements, like rolling over in bed, have become a chore as she is pretty uncomfortable, and carrying your baby—now fully grown—in her belly is exhausting. This means that there are several tasks to tackle to prepare your home for the arrival of your baby. These are things you can do while she takes a much-deserved break and will allow you to show off your handyman skills and what a hands-on hero you are.

Make room in the fridge. If you can pump and store breastmilk, extras will need to be kept fresh while your baby is still on a liquid diet. You'll also need space to store the prepared meals that caring friends or neighbors might drop off when you come home from the hospital.

Sterilizing bottles and the breast pump now will save time when you need these for the first time. Later on, you'll get so comfortable cleaning these that you can do it with your eyes closed—quite literally at times. But you may be insecure about whether you've done it right the first couple of times. You should sterilize the nipples and bottles before first-time use by leaving them in boiling water for about five minutes. After that, they only need a good wash and rinse with hot soapy water.

After the baby shower - if you haven't had one already - I can assure you that you'll already have piles of new clothes. You didn't think that laundry would pile up before the baby even arrived, did you? Has any of it been washed yet? If not, do so now. Remove all packaging, tags, labels, and anything that can scratch your baby's sensitive skin, then give it a good wash. This way, you can be sure that these items contain no excess dye or anything else that can irritate that incredibly delicate and sensitive skin.

Are you expecting family or friends to stay over after you bring your baby home? Stock up on all the necessary toiletries, and be sure that there is clean linen and towels. However, don't feel required to say yes to visitors. A grandparent may be staying over to help you out as per a previous agreement, but this is a hectic time in your lives, and if you're not ready for visitors, you have no obligation to have them stay over. Our large extended family visited within hours of our children's births. While we were comfortable with this then, many people ask for no visitors until upwards of a month postpartum. There is no definitive time frame for everyone. Discuss your comfort level and intentions with your partner, and you do you! Although you'll be quite tired after delivery, your exhaustion will pale compared to the mother's. It's time to play bouncer, uphold your intentions regarding visitors, and safeguard your precious new family.

A checklist can also include tasks like whether you're stocked up on frozen food and essentials like toilet paper. Do you have all your baby will need? Try to be so prepared that there is no need to rush to the store daily.

Is the house baby-proof? Sure, your baby is pretty stationary for the first few months, but what about after that? Are the toxic chemicals still stored under the kitchen sink within reach once your baby starts to crawl? Pack these things on safe heights now so that it's already done.

The last thing on this list is to target the red zones. What? The red zones are those spots in every home that endures a lot of exposure to germs and bacteria. Doorknobs, sinks, toilets, sponges, countertops, cell phones, light switches, and faucet handles are all on the list. Again, your baby won't have contact with these parts of the home, but you and your visitors will, and you can collect germs and bacteria on your hands from here and carry them to your baby. So, give it a good clean. You can even have sanitizing wipes on hand to keep wiping these spots regularly to limit the accumulation of nasties.

Tips to Induce Labor

One crucial thing you can do as a supportive and caring partner - who is keen on making the life of the woman carrying his baby easier - is to help her to induce labor once the time comes. Babies, especially the first, take their time to arrive, and your partner likely doesn't want to wait any longer. Most women past their due date have only one wish—to get the baby out of them. So, what can you do?

There are actually quite a few things that can induce labor when your baby is ready to be born. Take a walk together. First, exercise and fresh air will relieve stress, but they can also kick off the labor process.

You can also jumpstart labor through nipple stimulation. When you do this, the body produces oxytocin which can cause both the expression of milk and the uterus to contract.

Castor oil triggers the release of prostaglandin, which helps the cervix to ripen and so start labor. But take this advice only under the guidance of your doctor or midwife, as you can easily take too much of this oil.

Although acupuncture may seem like an abstract science, it absolutely works. If this is of interest to you, pay a visit to a licensed acupuncturist.

You can also consider acupressure if your partner doesn't feel like being punctured with dozens of needles. It may help her to go into labor or, at the very least, release some tension.

And then there is sex. As mentioned before, if a baby is ready to be born, sex can aid labor through the beneficial hormones released and the contraction of the uterus during the climax. Your semen also contains prostaglandin, which helps to ripen the cervix. Don't have sex if her water has broken because of the risk of exposing the baby to infection.

We seemed to have figured out the secret formula for Dani's body to induce labor. Again, these things don't necessarily kick off the process but definitely assist things already in motion. In the 24 hours leading up to the birth of all three of our children, we happened to have walked a mile or so, had sex, and I had applied acupressure to specific "labor-inducing" points on her body. In fact, with our last baby, we were sitting on the couch watching TV, and Dani had asked me to rub her feet and given instructions on finding labor-inducing spots. The literal second I had found the correct 'SP6' point (an acupressure point located on the ankle), we both witnessed an audible pop as if it were muffled underwater. Her water had broken, and we were in the hospital preparing for the birth of our last child within a few hours.

As with any other health advice, always consult your doctor before practicing certain labor-inducing techniques to ensure the safety of your pregnancy.

Final *Must-Have* Conversations

Once you return from the hospital, it may be harder to find time to sit down as a couple and have a decent uninterrupted conversation. As you're in the third trimester, it will be wise to discuss the following topics now, as well as labor, to be sure you're ready for what lies ahead.

At this point, you've already formed a bond with your doctor, midwife, or doula. But do you want to record the birth, have pictures taken, fill the room with music, and will your partner do this with or without medication?

You'll also have to discuss intervention contingencies. Birth is a natural process, but there are a lot of things that can go wrong. The best way to clear your mind from these concerns so that you both can fully immerse yourself in the wonder of birth is to have these discussions before labor so that you both know what the process would look like if something unexpected happened.

Other topics include where your partner and baby would be the most comfortable the first couple of days or weeks after birth. What support system do you have in place if postpartum depression kicks in and your partner is struggling? Who can you turn to for support if this happens or if you feel similar depression or anxiety?

Also, discuss what intimacy might look like after birth. Again, your partner may take a while to be ready for lovemaking, but simply having time carved out to be alone is a wonderful way to be intimate and reconnect after this huge event in your life.

I'll be capturing many of these steps in the next chapter, where we'll explore how to create a birth plan.

The Hospital Bag

This is the holy grail of all bags. The single most important piece of luggage you'll ever have. It can be a lifeline when you are at the hospital. So together, you need to master the balance of packing all you'll need while not wasting space with unnecessary items. Often, it s your partner who will be packing the bag, and you only need to remember to grab it on your way to the hospital but believe me, it's good that you, too, know what is in there since you'll be her go-to helper. You'll also have needs at the hospital or birthing center.

First of all, when should this be packed? It's good to be prepared from at very least the eighth month onwards. If you are a serial over-packer like my wife and I, then utilizing two bags, one for delivery and one for after the baby is born, can help reduce the number of items you bring into the hospital upon check-in. A quick run out to the car for the postpartum or sleeping necessities will do the trick.

It's best to have a checklist to ensure that nothing is forgotten. What should go into the bag?

- The necessary paperwork - Birth plan, ID, hospital paperwork, insurance card, and copies of medical records

- A bathrobe - to pace around in during labor

- Warm fuzzy socks

- Slippers or flip-flops - for both of you if you are able to spend the night in the hospital too

- Lip balm

- Body lotion or massage oil - a massage can go a long way to relieve pain and discomfort during labor

- Pillows - the hospital will provide you with a few pillows, but you may both prefer ones from home. You'll want the best possible sleep while you're there

- An eye mask, earplugs, or white noise machine - makes sleeping easier in a strange environment

- Relaxing entertainment like a card game - labor can be a process of hurrying up and waiting. Pack something to kill time while waiting on your baby

- A nursing-friendly nightgown or two - for her stay after labor

- Underwear - the hospital will provide heavy-duty maternity pads and disposable mesh underwear for postpartum bleeding; however, she may have others she would prefer to use instead. Comfortable bras or nursing bras

- Toiletries - even though you may need less, be sure to pack some items for yourself, too, as you'll also want to freshen up during your stay

- Phone, camera, and chargers

- Glasses or contact lenses

- Clothes to go home in and for during your stay - remember a change of clothes for you as well as something comfortable to sleep in

- A warm layer like a sweater or sweatshirt - regardless of the outside temperature, hospitals tend to run a bit cold. Your baby will also need clothes to go home in and, of course, booties to keep its feet warm

- Snacks and drinks - those vending machine purchases sure add up quickly, so bring a decent handful of healthy alternatives

- Reference books or notes - made during antenatal classes

- A comfortable blanket for you to sleep with - the extra hospital blankets aren't always the best

This sounds like a lot, but there are also things you don't need to pack.

- Too many baby clothes - the hospital will provide you with onesies for the baby. Big bonus, because you don't have to bring anything home to wash

- Any valuable items

- Full-blown meals

- Too much bedding - the hospital will provide the basics

- Hair dryers - many hospitals provide these, but be sure to ask if this is an important item to you or your partner

- Too many grooming products - bring your must-haves, but complementary ones are often supplied

- Too much entertainment - other than a possibly lengthy delivery, you won't have as much downtime during your stay as you think. Between extremely short bouts of sleep, rounds of visitors, and assisting your partner with her needs as well as the baby's, you won't have much free time

Two more things you can take care of are ensuring there is enough gas in the car and that the car seat is properly installed according to the manufacturer's guidelines.

Overcoming Possible Complications

Preparation is better than panic. Let's not stew on the possible negatives for too long. Instead, we'll ease potential worries and concerns by reviewing and readying ourselves for certain scenarios.

Preeclampsia

I've mentioned preeclampsia before, but let's just pause here for a moment to learn exactly what it is. Preeclampsia is a serious condition linked to high blood pressure and possible kidney damage in your partner. The scariest attribute of this concern is that it can sometimes go undetected as it can have no noticeable symptoms. So, it's usually detected during routine visits to your doctor.

Some of the symptoms of preeclampsia are severe headaches, shortness of breath as fluids may gather in the lungs, nausea, vomiting, a drop in the level of platelets in the blood, liver problems, and excess protein in the blood. A more obvious sign is a sudden onset of severe edema or swelling of the extremities, particularly in the legs and feet.

As a dad, you'll have to deal with your concerns about the health of your partner and baby, but you'll also have to be there for your partner. Her distress will also exceed being merely physical. She might feel like she failed, and it's important to remind her that what happened is completely normal. A lot of support will also be necessary after birth. She may have to stay longer in the hospital and not be able to have as much contact with your baby as she wants. These are all factors that can make her more vulnerable to depression. Listen to her, be there for her, take care of her. She has been through a lot, physically and emotionally, and she will likely feel drained.

After going home, the doctor will ask you to monitor her blood pressure for a while and keep an eye on postpartum depression. Remember that you can also only do the best you can, but you'll be able to do more if you take care of yourself too. Just be there, take responsibilities off her shoulders, understand how she feels, get her the medical attention she needs, and spoil her by cooking her favorite meal. The last couple of months were rough; now, it's time to recover and grow together as a family.

Placenta Complications

The most common complication with the placenta is placenta abruption. Still, that said, it remains a rather uncommon concern entailing the placenta coming loose from the uterus wall too soon. Your baby relies on a proper connection between the placenta and uterus as it feeds and gets oxygen this way, so if this bond is jeopardized, it can decrease the necessary supply to your baby. This concern can happen rather suddenly, and it needs immediate treatment to reduce risk to the mother and baby. Symptoms to be wary of are

- Pain in the abdomen and back

- Contractions in the uterus accompanied by tenderness or pain in this area

- Vaginal bleeding, while this may not always occur

The risks for the mother are that her body can go into shock due to blood loss, blood clotting problems, and she may need a blood transfusion. There is also the risk of kidney failure and a hysterectomy if doctors can't control her bleeding.

The condition also puts your baby at risk and can result in premature labor or stillbirth as your baby isn't getting enough oxygen. The lack of nutrients will also slow down growth.

This type of concern usually goes along with chronic high blood pressure if it occurred during a previous pregnancy, a blow or fall on the abdomen, or if there is an infection in the uterus. It can also be caused by high-risk circumstances like cocaine use, preeclampsia, and when the mother is over 40.

This isn't a medical concern that can be prevented. Even if you do everything right, it can still occur but know that it isn't a common concern, and the condition can be managed very well with the correct intervention early on.

Just support your partner physically and emotionally, reassure her that it wasn't her fault, and listen to her needs.

Preterm Labor

When your partner goes into labor before 37 weeks, it's considered preterm labor. While your baby is already well developed, it isn't quite ready yet to exit the womb, and there may be certain complications. When this happens, getting medical care as quickly as possible is vital. Your partner will be monitored at the hospital, and doctors will likely use progesterone to prevent preterm birth for as long as possible.

Preterm births can be caused by infection or a shortened cervix, and the mother is more likely to have another preterm birth if a previous pregnancy already ended this way. Other causes include too much amniotic fluid, the mother's age, race, or ethnicity—this is more common in black and Hispanic women—stress, or if your baby has a congenital disability.

Symptoms to be aware of are low, dull back pain, spotting or light bleeding, cramps in the abdominal area, a sensation of pressure on the pelvis, and light contractions. Again, you can't control everything, and even if you and your partner do everything right according to every bit of medical advice you've ever received, it can still happen. Yet, maintaining a healthy lifestyle, attending regular doctor's visits, managing any chronic conditions, and avoiding any risky behavior or substances, can aid in prevention.

Know that we live in an amazing time with unbelievably advanced medical practices. Even babies born very prematurely can fully develop and still live normal and healthy lives with the proper postpartum care.

Secret Dad Tips

As a dad, it's always good to have a good plan up your sleeve.

Tip #7:

Plan for your child's financial future: Your partner is busy with a thousand things linked to nesting, looking after herself, still managing her life as she is probably continuing to work, and preparing for birth. Financial matters may not be at the forefront of her mind right now. This is something you could take care of — setting up a savings account for your child.

There are several benefits linked to doing this so early on. You'll have enough time to save quite a bit if you start early. It will help you to achieve specific financial goals for your child, there are some tax benefits to it, and it will force you to become more financially keen.

Most banks offer different savings account options for babies, and you can pop into your local bank to explore what options they have on offer. While you can explore the possibilities pre-birth, you'll need your baby's birth certificate to open the actual account.

 You can also start saving for your baby's education by opening an account to pay for their studies. Education has become very expensive, and it will benefit you to prepare for this expense now. Invest your money wisely to reap great returns on your investment, ensuring your unborn child's education.

Remember that you'll have to do this every time you add a new member to your family so that every child has sufficient financial provisions.

Tip #8:

Bond with your baby before birth: It can be frustrating at times when you wish to interact more with your unborn child to build a bond, and you simply can't. However, there are a couple of things you can do to form this bond while your baby is still in the womb.

Touch your partner's belly. By the third trimester, I was very comfortable touching Dani's belly and talking to our baby. Spending all this time so close to our child made me feel like I was connected to our son before birth. Also, your baby will feel positive and intimate vibes when you and your partner spend these close moments with your child. They can hear and recognize your voice during the third trimester. When our son was born, he would whip his head up and crane his head on that tiny little neck until he found me in the room. He recognized my voice whenever I talked. Even when he was fussy or tired, my voice soothed him. It's a magnificent feeling when you internalize that your child knows who you are even in the womb.

Once your baby is born, it's important to enjoy as much skin-to-skin contact as possible, as this, too, will strengthen your bond.

FAQs

Q: When will our baby be ready to breathe outside the womb?

A: Lung development is one of the most serious concerns when it appears your baby is coming early. From 38 weeks onwards, your baby's lungs are fully developed, and it will be able to breathe on its own. However, many babies are born earlier than 37 weeks, and with the right care and a little initial help, they do fine too.

Q: Why is my partner constantly feeling hot?

A: The first assumption is often that she is getting a fever, but in fact, it's just your baby radiating heat, causing your partner to feel hot often.

Q: My partner notices increased hair growth on her arms and legs. Is that normal?

A: Yes, this hair growth is caused by the high level of human growth hormones in her body. It will return to normal after giving birth.

Journal Prompts

Have you been keeping up with journaling? It must be evident that you must be emotionally, physically, and mentally strong to keep yourself upright and be there for your partner to lean on for any of her needs. So, don't neglect taking care of yourself by eating a healthy diet, getting as much sleep as possible, and remaining fit. Also, look after your emotional health. Keeping a journal, unburdening yourself from any negative emotions, and gathering your thoughts will surely be helpful.

So, here are three more prompts to keep you going during this part of the journey.

- What am I looking forward to the most about bringing our baby home?

- What scares me the most about the birthing process lying ahead?

- What made me appreciate my partner the most during this entire pregnancy?

Conclusion

I keep all my jokes in a dad-a-base.

Yep, store those puppies up because it's nearly crunch time. So, let's help you dive into the labor-intensive (pun intended) task of discussing and creating a birth plan.

Chapter 8

A Plan for Labor and Birth

There's a whole birthing plan, but what is the plan other than to get it out? I mean, there isn't an option to kind of keep it in, is there? So, I'm assuming my plan is to get it out. But apparently, there's more to the plan than that. I don't know what that is.
—Keira Knightley

R emember that your birth plan can change whenever you feel the need to make certain adjustments. Putting a plan for this day onto paper may feel like jumping the gun, but planning ahead is more about knowing what to expect, being ready for anything, and realizing what to do when things don't go as planned. So, let's figure it out.

Creating a Birth Plan

Failing to plan is planning to fail, right? While the lack of proper planning won't stop the birth of your baby from happening, having a well-thought and structured plan in place will surely make the entire process easier and far more enjoyable for yourself and your partner.

Before digging any deeper, I want to put your mind at ease by confirming that there is no right or wrong birth plan. It's either a case of having such a plan in place or not. Even if you choose not to have a plan, it's also okay. Falling back on such a plan just brings some peace and certainty to the chaos often surrounding birth.

The plan can be a complex plan stipulating almost every controllable detail about the birthing process, or it can be quite simple, merely providing a guideline of how you and your partner would like the day to play out.

Remember that you're not married to this plan. As circumstances change, the plan can change. But what the plan will do besides giving you guys more clarity on what needs to happen on this important day is that it gives your partner a voice in what is happening to her body when she is in labor. It also gives you the confidence to advocate for her when needed.

Heading into the third trimester is a perfect time to begin drafting such a plan.

Getting Started

All right, you are all amped to get that birth plan into writing, but where do you start? What do you need to include in this plan? These questions can be daunting as you're essentially planning for an event for which you have no idea what it will be like when it first happens — I'm speaking to first-time dads now.

Does your partner have a clear idea of how she wants to give birth? Not all women have such clarity on what they prefer for the birthing process, and a lot of women simply follow their doctor's instructions. But it can be that your partner thoroughly researched different birthing options and wants to make her preference clear in this document. If you chose to attend any antenatal classes or did some reading on various birthing methods like Lamaze, hypnobirthing, or other labor techniques, she likely has a vision of how she imagines the delivery process going. This will be a great place to start.

Capture all the important things to you both and what you would like to happen on this day.

If you choose to write this plan by hand, ensure your handwriting is legible—you're not the only person who will have to read this plan. Another option is to type and print it for clarity.

Make a few copies of this plan as they can easily get misplaced on this sometimes chaotic day.

Helpful points to include in the plan are:

- Where you want to birth your baby

- Preferred positions during labor and birthing, including whether or not she would like to labor in a tub

- Ways you can help to make labor easier for her

- The ambiance you would like to create in the labor room - i.e., soothing music, essential oils or battery-operated candles

- All individuals that are part of your support network

- Any cultural birthing factors you want to include

- What pain relief options your partner is comfortable with

- What pain relief options she wants to avoid

- A list of massage techniques you know offer pain relief to your partner (pro-tip: learn how to apply counterpressure appropriately in case she experiences back labor)

- Will you be cutting the umbilical cord?

- Whether or not you will request delayed cord clamping

- How much skin-to-skin contact you would like with your baby

- If it's a boy, do you want him to be circumcised? Will this be done straight away?

- Whether or not your partner is planning to breastfeed

- How you can support your partner after birth

- What you want to happen with your baby just after it's born

***

Your ***FREE BONUS*** includes a **birth plan template!** Remember to download it for your bump-to-baby 'To Dos', checklists, journal prompts, and other important printables!

***

At this point, you've already determined whether you're relying on a doctor, midwife, or doula. So, it would be beneficial to share this information with them too. While you're free to share your birth plan with anyone, every professional involved in the birthing process must know what your birth plan entails.

Parenting is all about planning and then adjusting your plans to adapt to the ever-changing circumstances linked to having kids. Later on, you'll learn that everything can change in the blink of an eye with kids. For example, you may plan to have a lovely day out with the family, only to wake up with an uneasy and fussy baby not ready to go anywhere. These unexpected changes start from day one — time to assume the superpower of adaptability.

I am referring to unexpected changes like hearing you have a breech baby. Having a breech baby means that your baby isn't turning into the position it's supposed to lie in for natural birth. Instead of lying with their heads down in the pelvic area, they lie with their bottoms or feet towards the birth canal.

Doctors can typically determine whether your baby is breech around week 36 of pregnancy, but it can also happen much later—like when in labor. Babies more likely to breech are twins or when there is too little or too much amniotic fluid. The shape of the uterus or the presence of growths can also impact it when your baby has an abnormality that keeps them from turning, when your baby is born preterm, or when the placenta covers the cervix, which also keeps the baby from moving into position for birth.

While having a breech baby won't impact the pregnancy, it sure will mean that all your plans of having a natural birth will likely have to go out the window. Many doctors consider it unsafe for a breech baby to be born naturally, and it will put immense strain on your partner. However, some health care providers will be willing to still opt for a natural birth when it's a breech baby as they then turn the baby in the right position while still in the womb, but there will be heavy factors and possible complications to consider. As parents, you need to decide whether you want to put yourselves and your baby under this pressure or whether you prefer to opt for a C-section.

Plans to Ensure Your Partner of Your Support

You'll likely drive your wife to the hospital or birthing center. By now, you know which hospital that would be, so you can determine the shortest route. Knowing that you've got an efficient route planned and are ready to support her will bring her a great deal of comfort.

If you didn't already do so during the antenatal class, Make arrangements for you both to tour the hospital where you plan to give birth. Kill two birds with one stone and coordinate with your pre-registration appointment. Touring the department and labor rooms will help you envision what it will be like and where to go and help you feel more familiar with the setting. This visit will leave you with the comforting sense that you're prepared.

During this visit, you can also ask all the questions you may have about giving birth at the facility. The following are some of the most common questions in need of answers:

- What amenities do they offer?

- What are the medical services available at the site?

- What laboring equipment or amenities do they provide? I.e., a laboring stool, bathtub, or exercise ball

- What can you expect from the facility and the team?

- Find out about their rules regarding visitors.

- How long will your baby be with you after delivery?

- Can you stay there overnight with your partner?

- Will they offer breastfeeding support?

Another thing to consider in your birth plan is your action plan if your partner's water breaks. Only about 15% of women experience a spontaneous membrane rupture. Still, consider what you'll do, what she needs to do, and the best way to support her. For example, she can shower while you ensure everything is packed before heading to the hospital. What are your plans for childcare if this isn't your first? I strongly suggest having a plan 'b' in case your first option doesn't pan out. You can also support her by having a relaxing conversation or listening to soothing music to remain calm and centered when her contractions begin.

In Case of Sudden Changes

All may appear to go perfectly fine until your healthcare provider tells you that it's necessary for an emergency Cesarean or an epidural. I'm not saying it will happen, but you're on the final stretch of being the best hen in this pregnancy, and it's necessary to fulfill your duties. In this case, the duty is to be prepared for anything.

Ideally, an emergency C-section should not take any longer than 30 minutes from the moment the doctor makes this call until your baby is taking its first breath. That said, it can sometimes take longer as it's a much larger procedure requiring far more people to be on staff and available. This will only happen if either your partner's or your baby's health is at risk if you proceed with a natural birth.

Even if you have planned to have a C-section, the situation can still become an emergency. Basically, there are three types of C-sections:

Scheduled C-sections: Together with your healthcare provider, you've decided that this is the best option to give birth to your child, and the procedure is typically scheduled up to a week before your predicted due date. Your doctor may have you schedule a c-section if you have had previous complicated deliveries or previous c-sections, are expecting more than one baby, or have other risks such as high maternal age or genetic issues with mom or baby.

Unplanned C-sections: This occurs when your doctor identifies certain causes for concern, like a breech baby, and veers off the plan of having a vaginal birth a couple of hours, days, or weeks before birth. It's not an emergency situation, though—just a last-minute change of plans.

Emergency C-sections: Occurs when there is a sudden change in the condition of the pregnancy, and your medical team needs to get the baby out quickly.

There are a couple of reasons why an emergency C-section becomes necessary. Your partner may be too exhausted from a long birth already, and she has no strength left to push the baby out. The baby might have shifted into a different position making natural birth too hard, or there could've been changes in the baby's or mom's health, like a drop in blood pressure. Another concern is when the umbilical cord becomes knotted or tangled around your baby or when the placenta makes it difficult to give birth. This could cause hypoxia: a lack of sufficient oxygen to the baby.

For many parents, this sudden change in plans comes as quite a shock, and what makes it worse is that your partner's recovery will look much different than from normal birth. Now, you'll have to consider things like stitches opening up, the possibility of wound infection, heavy bleeding and blood loss, blood clots, and not reacting well to the anesthesia. The chances of having a v-bac (vaginal birth after cesarean) are much slimmer.

Induction

Usually, it's okay to go over your due date, even by a couple of days, but there will come a point when your healthcare professional may decide that having the pregnancy go on for longer will be putting your partner or baby at risk. At that point, they'll induce labor. It can also be that the water already broke, but the contractions are still lacking.

The process requires merely the insertion of a prostaglandin gel into the vagina, which helps to ripen the cervix and will kickstart the contractions.

If the prostaglandin gel didn't quite do the trick, then she will likely be administered an i.v. with pitocin, a synthetic form of the hormone oxytocin, which stimulates uterine contractions.

Pain Management

Don't ever judge any woman who has initially planned on taking no pain meds during labor and then changes her mind last minute. Just don't. The pain and exhaustion she is experiencing as she brings your child into the world is unfathomable.

Your partner can choose to fall back onto several types of pain relief. There is gas or air, which is a special blend of oxygen and nitrous called Entonox, which helps relieve pain. While it may make mom feel lightheaded, it does not affect your baby.

A specific pain medication, pethidine, can also be injected. It's usually into the thigh and takes about 20 minutes to kick in. It can make your partner feel woozy, and if it's given too close to birth, it can affect your baby's breathing. So, it's best to choose this option earlier on.

Epidurals are probably the most commonly used form of pain relief. It's a local anesthetic numbing the nerves running from the birth canal to the brain. It can make your partner feel drowsy. It's also long-lasting and is meant to be effective throughout the entire birthing process. However, it requires an anesthetist as the injection needs to be made into the spine. Depending on the type of epidural injected, your partner may be unable to use her legs for a while until it has worn off. As you need a specialist for this option and your baby's heart rate needs to be monitored throughout, this pain relief isn't available to births outside the hospital. It's also an option you should plan for in advance. The entire process requires about

15 minutes to set up and then about another 15 minutes to work, so if it's too close to giving birth, you may not be able to choose this option.

An epidural will take away the pain but not the contractions. It will affect the labor, but with a medical team by your side, they'll guide your partner exactly when she needs to push.

It's important to remind her during labor that her health, safety, and comfort are just as vital as your baby's. She should not shy away from necessary medical interventions because she regards your baby's life as more important than her own.

The Different Stages of Labor

Labor is a lengthy process with several stages.

Latent stage: The cervix is getting ready for birth by becoming softer and thinner to make birth easier. There may be some contractions far apart. The best thing you can do is to help your partner feel peaceful by creating a tranquil environment at home. You can also call your doctor or midwife to inform them of the progress. Usually, if you've had a normal and healthy pregnancy up to this point and are past the 37-week mark, you'll be advised to stay home. This phase can last a couple of hours to even days.

Water Breaking: You don't have to rush off to the hospital when the water breaks. Movies have instilled an entirely skewed image of how long it takes from the moment the water breaks until the baby is born. Breaking of water is merely the first sign that your partner is going into labor, and while it can certainly speed some things up, it can still be hours before her contractions begin. Your doctor will ask you to call if and when her water breaks. They will instruct you on what risks to look out for and what time frame they will want you to report to the birth center.

When to Go to the Hospital: It's normal to want to jump into the car straight away upon the first contraction. Don't. Rather wait until contractions last for a minute and are about five minutes apart. Until then, your partner can still labor in the comfort of your home. It also depends on how far away you stay from the hospital. A great task to keep your mind at ease and present is to be in charge of tracking and timing the contractions. Both of your trains of thought are likely to be derailed with so much anticipation and infinite 'what ifs.' Utilize an app to help reign it all in and stay focused on this miraculous experience. Only once your partner has dilated more than 4 cm will they admit her and continue with the labor and delivery of your baby. You won't know how far she has dilated. So, keep track of her contractions.

1st stage: The first stage is considered the onset of labor, and the cervix has dilated up to 4cm. The contractions are becoming more regular and stronger.

Now, the next recognized stage starts only when the cervix has opened up completely, but don't be fooled by that. The transition stage from when the hospital will admit your partner to actual labor is surely the hardest and most exhausting part for you both. Especially to get to 7cm can be a battle, often taking hours, during which you need to be there for your partner the entire time.

2nd stage: Your partner has a fully opened cervix, meaning it's about 10 cm wide, and the muscles are tightening and relaxing to push your baby out.

3rd stage: This stage occurs when your baby is already born, but now your partner will have to deliver the placenta. The delivered placenta and membranes are called afterbirth.

Delayed stages: During any stage of labor, it can happen that the stage is happening very slowly in comparison to the normal expectation. If this occurs, your medical team may step in and take precautionary measures and gradually speed up the process through interventions like introducing pitocin. If these delays are still present during the second stage of birth, it may be necessary to opt for assisted birth via forceps, a vacuum, or a C-section.

Hastening stages: occurs when your baby needs to be born quickly, as there are certain concerns, and your medical team wants to get the baby out as quickly as possible.

Understanding the Terms

Another way to shine in your supportive role and to be truly present for your partner is by having a clear understanding of some of the terms you'll hear during labor. For your benefit, I've compiled a short glossary of terms to master this trimester and explanations of what to expect.

Mucus plug: The mucus plug is about 1-2 inches long and 1-2 tablespoons in volume. It's sticky, stringy, and jelly-like and is clear or off-white, sometimes tinged with blood, and without any smell. It usually stays in place until after 37 weeks, but some people may lose theirs only a few days before birth. It's possible to lose this gradually or with one big blob. If she experiences this before 37 weeks, she may need to speak to her doctor, as this is part of the labor process.

Episiotomy: If you're ever feeling sorry for yourself as a dad, I want you to think about an episiotomy and be grateful that it isn't you giving birth. The term refers to a procedure where doctors make a cut from the vaginal opening toward the anus if the opening isn't large enough for the baby to exit. At first, your healthcare provider will allow your baby's head to stretch the vaginal tissue, but if it's still too tight for the baby to exit, it may need to be cut wider open. Episiotomies are no longer a routine procedure since studies have shown that recovering from a naturally healed tear improves tissue health down the line. However, if the doctor is worried that there may be a risk of nerve damage due to excessive tearing, he or she may still perform the procedure. The provider will stitch up the cut once your baby is born and the placenta has also been delivered. If your partner already had an epidural, the doctor will make this cut without any further injections, but without an epidural, they'll first administer a numbing shot into the area.

Dilation and Cervical Effacement: Also referred to as ripening, effacement is the thinning of the cervix in preparation for delivery. During effacement, the cervix starts out more than an inch thick and ends up paper-thin.

Dilation is a measurement of the diameter of the cervix in centimeters, indicating an opening and readiness for your baby to be born.

Pitocin: Remember the hormone oxytocin and how it plays a vital role in uterine contractions? Pitocin is a synthetic version of this hormone used in IV to induce labor.

Augmentation of labor: An intervention helps labor progress more rapidly. Pitocin (a synthetic form of the oxytocin hormone) is often used to make contractions stronger or rupture the membranes.

Placenta: The placenta is an organ that develops during pregnancy to provide oxygen and nutrients to your baby through the attached umbilical cord. It also removes the waste products from the baby's blood. It does this by attaching itself to the uterine wall.

Epidural: It's an anesthesia used to numb the nerves in your lower back. The numbing occurs from the injection site down to the feet, making it an effective form of pain management during labor. While it allows your partner to feel pressure, it will eliminate most pain, making the process much easier for her.

Cesarean: A C-section is a procedure where an incision is made into the abdomen and uterus to remove the baby when a vaginal birth is complicated or impossible.

Crowning: During labor, when the baby's head is visible within the external vaginal opening.

What Happens to Her Body During Labor?

It helps to better understand the physiological processes of labor.

During the third trimester, your partner will experience Braxton Hicks contractions. These are basically test runs for labor, but they can also be considered forerunners of the process. The uterus is a muscle, so by going through the motions of practice contractions, it's quite literally toning and gaining strength for a rigorous job ahead. Before she can go into labor, a process called cervical ripening needs to take place first. Just like a fruit grows softer as it ripens, the cervix also becomes softer during the ripening process.

If this doesn't happen, it can't dilate as necessary for birth. Several hormonal changes are responsible for the ripening process, causing a reduction in collagen and an increase in glycosaminoglycans and hyaluronic acid. The process also entails the breakdown of cervical connection tissue, causing the cervix to become softer. Cervical ripening either occurs naturally or can be accomplished artificially using prostaglandins or misoprostol.

What causes the uterus to contract? Gradually, progesterone levels drop in relation to estrogen, causing greater excitability of the uterine muscles. As the baby grows larger, it also stretches the uterus, making it easier to contract with these muscles. We can't talk about contractions without mentioning oxytocin. We've already touched on this, mentioning that it helps initiate contractions. During pregnancy, there is a low number of oxytocin receptors in the uterine muscles, but as the pregnancy progresses and especially toward the end, these receptors increase drastically in numbers. This makes the uterus much more sensitive to the presence of oxytocin when the pituitary gland releases it. The entire process is called the

Ferguson reflex. And that, dear dad-to-be, is what labor and contractions are all about on a physiological level.

Multiple Babies

When you're expecting multiple babies, birth can bring about greater complexities, and there will likely be a greater need for access to more medical equipment. So, planning to give birth at a hospital or any other medical facility may be best.

It's a common practice in the field of medicine that multiple babies are born a little bit earlier than a singleton. Twins with their own placentas will usually be induced around 37-38 weeks, while identical twins sharing a placenta will be induced around 36-37 weeks. This is even earlier if your twins share a placenta and amniotic sac - here, we're looking at 32-36 weeks.

If you're expecting twins and have had a healthy pregnancy, vaginal birth is still very much on the table if your partner is up for it and your doctor is supportive. Otherwise, it will have to be a C-section.

If your babies were born premature, they'd likely spend time in the NICU (neonatal intensive care unit), where they'll be monitored and cared for until they're strong enough to go home with you. Doctors try to discharge both babies at the same time, but if one is stronger than the other, that won't be possible, and you may have to spend some time commuting between home and the hospital to care for both your babies. This can, of course, make it somewhat harder to settle in after birth and is something you should prepare for, not only to take care of yourself but also to support your partner during this challenging time.

Take note that when you're having multiple babies, breastfeeding is still a possibility. Until you're used to feeding them, it's advised that you feed them separately to ensure that they both get the individual attention they need.

Another factor to consider is that postnatal depression is more likely to occur when you've had multiple babies. While getting the right care will bring you both the relief you need, you'll also have to be there for each other, physically and emotionally, during this tumultuous time.

Secret Dad Tip

Tip #9:

Check your employee benefits: If you haven't done so yet, there is no more time to delay - you need to check your employee benefits regarding paternity leave. It has become more common over recent decades for men to leave during the first 12 weeks of their baby's birth. This number has risen from only 7.5% in the 1970s to an astounding 66.5% today. So, take the time you need to be there for your family (Scherer, 2021).

FAQs

Q: What would my role be as my partner's support person?

A: As the support person during labor, you need to help your partner remain focused and serene with breathing exercises. You also need to be familiar with her wishes regarding the use of medicine or any invasive procedures, as at some point, you might need to make certain calls on her behalf. You must also attend to her needs and be there for her physically and emotionally.

Q: Will they have to give my partner an episiotomy?

A: The time of routine episiotomies during birth is long gone, and today only about 13% of first-time mothers have to get an episiotomy to help their baby out. That said, though, the number of mothers who tear is much higher, and here you're looking at about 70% of all first-time mothers. If your baby is in distress, when your partner has been pushing for a while and still doesn't get your baby out, or if tearing is happening into the upper areas where the clitoris is, the doctor will have to cut her to prevent excess tissue damage.

Q: What if my partner doesn't get our baby out?

A: After a long labor process, your partner may become so tired that she no longer has the energy to push as hard as she should. The doctor may then assist with a tool. Two tools are used. These are the forceps and the vacuum extractor. Both devices can guide your baby while supporting your partner's pushing efforts.

Conclusion

What did the one ocean say to the other? Nothing. They just waved.

You, too, might be at a loss for words after spending time exploring the serious business of birth in as much detail as we just did. It all may have been more information than you wished to know, but you will be amazingly prepared for this last chapter of pregnancy and delivery. Remember, often in parenting, it's much easier to laugh over the challenges than to give in to frustration when you are rendered speechless. In the next chapter, it's time for an overview of the final amazing developmental wonders taking place in your partner's womb during the third trimester.

Chapter 9

The 3rd Trimester Breakdown

The third trimester—is probably the most challenging part of the pregnancy as your partner will be very uncomfortable and tired of carrying around the extra weight of your baby on top of being unable to sleep comfortably. It's a time when the anticipation of meeting your baby is fused with bouts of anxiety since the eminence of becoming parents is very real. You guys are almost there, but not yet. While all of this is taking place on an emotional and mental level, things are still happening on the physiological side too.

Week 28

 At this point, your baby has grown to the size of a coconut, is 15 inches (38 cm) long, and weighs 2.25 lbs (1 kg). All the organs necessary for life outside of the womb have been developed. While your baby will be able to see if born now, its eyes are still developing toward full maturity. It's also already starting to move into position for birth and is now lying almost diagonally, facing your partner's buttocks. The wonderful news is that at this stage, it can recognize sounds and will know your voice. While it will still be moving, it will rest more often now and be less active. As your baby's head

is typically facing downward at this point, your partner may have more heartburn, as every time the baby stretches its legs, it puts pressure on her diaphragm. There will be more days when your partner doesn't feel like a ray of sunshine as some of the first-trimester symptoms can reappear. I am specifically referring here to nausea and exhaustion. Now is the time to learn as much as possible about postpartum depression. You can also continue to have intercourse unless instructed otherwise by your doctor.

Week 29

 Imagine a large muskmelon, and then you'll know roughly what the size of your baby is now. It's 14.5 inches (36.8 cm) long and weighs 2.75 lbs (1.3 kg). Your baby's brain is currently going through a stage of rapid development, and therefore, its head is getting bigger too. Your baby will also be able to regulate its own temperature now, and its heart, muscles, and lungs are growing stronger. Your partner's breasts will become even larger in preparation for breastfeeding. She may experience a range of unpleasant symptoms like lack of breath as your baby puts pressure on her lungs. Varicose veins, constipation, and frequent urination are also daily symptoms she has to deal with, and the best you can do is to be there for her in every way she needs you. If you aren't sure how to anticipate her needs, then ask! Make it a point to also create time for yourself to be sure you have a full cup to pour from when your partner needs you. During this stage of pregnancy, you should also be more alert to notice any possible symptoms of health concerns and complications typical to the third trimester.

Week 30

Your baby is growing fast and is nearly the size of a napa cabbage. It's 15 inches (38 cm) long and weighs 3 lbs (1.36 kg). Your baby's eyes are now so well-developed that they can distinguish light and darkness and even begin to form a familiarity with their surroundings. All vital organs are well-developed, and now your baby will start rapidly gaining weight to protect the organs in place. As your baby grows so fast, the uterus will expand to make more room for it, and now your partner's ribcage will continue to expand as the belly moves up, taking more space and causing her greater discomfort. She'll likely feel more clumsy and has to be careful not to fall. Back pain, lack of sleep, cramps, and swollen feet will all be part of her life now. Hence, expect some mood swings and be exceptionally understanding and accommodating. Sure, you, too, are going through emotional stress and excitement, but at least your body isn't going through this strenuous marathon. Work together on your well-being by remaining active as much as possible and reducing your intake of high-sugar foods, as this will help to prevent gestational diabetes.

Week 31

By now, your baby has grown to 16 inches (41 cm) from head to toe and weighs about 3.3 lbs (1.5 kg). It's now the size of an English cucumber. It's plumping up with added fat underneath its skin to ensure a necessary layer of protection in preparation for birth. While the somersaults in the belly are ramping down —due to the limited space, it will still have plenty of kicks. Your baby's five senses are also developing fast. While all the symptoms of the previous week will prevail—until birth—your partner may also have colostrum leaking from her breasts, and Braxton Hicks contractions will keep you at the edge of your seat. If you both still enjoy intercourse and have your doctor's approval, go for it. It's time to finish the last tasks on your to-do list and be aware of Braxton Hicks contractions that last longer than usual, sudden headaches, facial swelling, blurred vision, and RUQ pain. RUQ stands for the right upper quadrant, referring to the location of the liver and gallbladder.

Week 32

In just a week, your baby has grown nearly an inch and weighs between 3.75 – 4 lbs (1.8-2 kg), and it's 16.7 inches (42.5 cm) tall and is the size of a head of romaine lettuce. As the fat underneath its skin becomes more compacted, your baby has now transitioned from translucent to almost opaque in appearance. Your partner's belly is now pointing towards her feet, much lower than before, leaving only about 13 cm or 5 inches between her belly button and the top of her baby bump. She'll experience the same symptoms, and you can be there for her to rub her feet, tell her how amazing she looks, lighten her burden of tasks in the house, and for emotional support. Be sure your birth plan is finalized (if you decide to have one), stay up to date with doctor's visits, maintain a healthy lifestyle, and pack your hospital bags. Remind her that there are only two months to go!

Week 33

Your baby is the size of a pineapple, roughly 15 - 17 inches (38 - 43 cm) tall, and weighs about 4.5 lbs (1.8 - 2 kg). Having an independent immune system, your baby is going from strength to strength inside its cozy womb. Persisting discomfort will wear your partner down, so expect that she won't feel her best. Now is not the time to plan any lavish social events but to consider her needs. Be aware of any signs of early labor, and together, be vigilant in contacting medical support if there are any concerns. It's better to be safe than sorry. It's also a good time to schedule a visit to your pediatrician's office, check in with them about any advice, and get to know this healthcare professional a little better.

Week 34

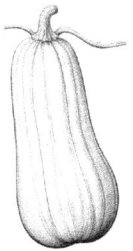

You've been pregnant for eight months already, and you'll be parents in a mere six weeks. Your baby's size is now similar to that of a butternut squash, 17.7 inches (45 cm) tall and weighing 4.7 lbs (2 kg) as it continues to grow rapidly. The only part of your baby's body that needs to become a bit stronger is its lungs. He or she still only has primitive alveoli, as the more mature lung structure has yet to form. Your partner may also feel your baby's hiccups which are now more common and prominent. While your partner may be looking in the mirror and noticing her stretch marks, swollen feet, and ankles, you can remind her how amazing she is for growing your tiny human and that she is as beautiful as ever. Share the mental load and remind her that everything will be perfectly fine. All the symptoms of third-trimester pregnancy are still present and will only worsen. It's a good time for quiet romantic candlelit dinners at home and to just enjoy being a couple for the last few weeks before you become parents.

Week 35

A luffa gourd is the closest description to your baby's current size, 5.3 - 5.5 lbs (2.4 - 2.5 kg) and 18 inches (45 cm) tall. As your baby's organs are now so well-developed and getting stronger, it's practicing and preparing for life outside the womb. Your little one is staying busy with workouts like kicking, grabbing, swallowing, and practicing its sucking reflexes for breastfeeding. If you're expecting a little boy, its testicles are now descending. Fat accumulation is also taking place rapidly, especially around the shoulder area. If you haven't invested in a full-body pillow for your partner yet, now is the time to do so. This will help her have the support she needs to get some rest. Prepare healthy, nutritious meals together and steer clear of anything that she notices aggravates her heartburn.

Week 36

 Four weeks to go! You're almost there, and while waiting for your baby to join you as a family, it's shooting up to the size of a papaya. It's 18 - 19 inches (45 - 48 cm) tall, weighing roughly 5.8 lbs (2.63 kg). Its circulation and the immune system are ready for the world outside the womb, and most systems are ready to support life. One system that still hasn't kicked into action is the digestive system which hasn't digested anything yet. An interesting fact is that a green sticky substance, called meconium, is inside its digestive system. This will be part of your baby's first poo together with any lanugo—the fine hair that covers its skin. This system will continue to develop until it's about two years old as it grows and balances its own gut microbiome. Your baby's skull is made up of soft bones that are still flexible to an extent, which eases the passage through the birth canal. Your partner will also notice a rapid weight increase, which can be alarming to anyone. Remind her that a lot of this weight is due to the baby's weight as well as the weight of the placenta, the extra blood that has been accumulating in her body over weeks, and the amniotic fluid. Any day now, your baby's head will drop down into the pelvis to be in position for birth. This will mean that your partner's belly will drop a little, freeing up her lungs and, in turn, possibly reducing her heartburn. This is also around when the mucus plug dislodges, either gradually or as one big blob.

Week 37

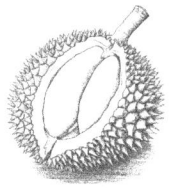

Now, your baby has the length of a durian. It's 19.1 inches (48.5 cm) tall and weighs 6.3 lbs (2.8 kg). Those days of comparing it to a poppy seed or a blueberry are long gone. During your doctor's visits, your healthcare provider will determine if your baby has taken the position for birth or whether there is any breaching. Your baby may be moving around a little to find its position, and these movements help with the thinning process of the uterine walls. It's now regularly practicing inhaling and exhaling amniotic fluid in preparation for breathing. Stretch mark cream is your partner's best friend, and you can earn some brownie points for rubbing it in for her (if she doesn't mind being touched, as the stretch marks can feel sensitive). It's also a way to spend intimate moments with her and be close to your baby. Your partner may experience swelling in new places, like extremities, and even her nose may increase in size. If your partner's nausea is bad, discuss solutions with your doctor. Take care that she doesn't dehydrate and also maintains a healthy nutritional intake. The pressure on her belly can also be much to handle, but standing on all fours will help. Be there to ensure she gets down and back up again safely. A nice soak in a deep tub or pool can support and lift the weight of the belly.

Week 38

Your baby is now about 19-20 inches (48.3 - 50.8 cm) tall, weighing about 6 - 7 lbs (2.7 - 3.2 kg), and is the size of a pumpkin! Most of your partner's pressure is now in her lower belly and pelvic floor, which also increases the pressure on her bladder, making bathroom breaks even more frequent. While the baby is in the home stretches of growing and building strength, this is the time to invest your attention in your partner's well-being. Her body has been through a lot over the past several months and has experienced so much discomfort. Some of the most common symptoms at this time in pregnancy are bloating, constipation (due to all the pressure on her bowels and slowed digestive system), feeling hot, tired, dizzy, experiencing headaches, having swollen hands and feet, and increased vaginal discharge. Sounds like fun, right? If your partner seems more needy or demanding, just ask yourself what you would be like if that were your body. It's ok to go above and beyond for her right now.

Week 39

 Imagine carrying a watermelon in your belly. That is the current size of your baby. It is roughly 19.5-20.5 inches (49.5 cm - 52 cm) tall and weighs about 6.5 - 8 lbs (2.9 - 3.6 kg). Your baby is now considered full-term, but development continues until birth. During the past month, its brain has developed by 30%, and its skin has turned white, regardless of ethnicity. It is still increasing the fat layer underneath its skin and has developed the ability of cell renewal. Your partner may feel more clumsy while the pressure in her lower pelvic area increases dramatically. At this stage, intercourse is still on the table if you both feel up to it. Have you discussed matters like intimacy after birth yet? Remember that recovery and mental health can look very different from how you may picture them. It's ok to reevaluate and re-discuss these topics after the baby comes as well.

Week 40

 Way to go! You've made it to full term and can now reflect on your journey with only one last step from meeting your baby. Your baby is now the size of, well, a newborn baby, weighs between 6.7 - 10 lbs (3-4.5 kg), and is 20.5 -21 in (48.3 - 54 cm) tall. Its bones have grown hard—except for the unfused plates in the skull, which still need to go through the birth canal. Your baby is ready for life outside the womb, and your due date is any moment now. A significant change taking place in your partner's body is cervix effacement or dilation in preparation for birth. She may also start to have diarrhea—yep, the complete opposite after battling for months with con-

stipation. At times, she may also experience pelvic pain as there is pressure on the nerve ends located in the area. Now is the time for relaxation—for both of you. Soon you'll be sleep-deprived parents, and I urge you to take the last couple of days to draw close to each other, be intimate—even if you aren't having sex —and just be there for each other emotionally.

Chapter 10

Bringing Life Into The World

*My mother groaned, my father wept, into the dangerous world,
I leapt.* —William Blake

This quote hits hard because a new parent fears everything. However, with basic knowledge and tips from a fellow parent, you'll do just fine. Nothing is ever as scary as the unknown, but knowledge is power. It's important to identify what to expect and how to recognize normal signs, symptoms, and behavior to remove the unpleasant sting of worries that can punch into your parenting expectations.

The big day is finally here, and while you're bursting with excitement, you may also be overflowing with concerns. To stop these fears from robbing you of the ultimate joy of becoming a parent, I'm sharing exactly what to expect when your baby is born.

By now, you're familiar with labor symptoms, when to head to the hospital, and what to expect. But labor and birthing are a process of hurry-up and wait, and there is a lot you can do to make labor easier for your partner. I'm specifically referring here to supporting her, helping her feel relaxed, working through the contractions, and supporting her emotional needs in between.

Birthing—Before, During, and After

Labor can be a much easier process if done in a soothing environment. What are the things that help your partner in labor to relax? Some preferred choices are background music of her choice (some may find this annoying, while it brings tranquility to others), having a focal point to zoom in on during contractions, massaging her back, utilizing creative imagery, progressive relaxation, or the obvious breathing exercises—this is just one of the many reasons attending those antenatal classes come in handy.

Of these techniques, there are three I would like to emphasize.

Massaging: There are different massage techniques that you can follow, but the key to success is to be gentle. Light circular motions on her abdomen can ease the pain of labor, while you can also massage her back, legs, shoulders, and feet. If she is experiencing back labor, you can apply firmer pressure with your fists on her lower back using steady circular strokes. Even her arms and thighs can benefit from long firm strokes, and who doesn't enjoy a head and neck massage? Soft pressure on her temples and the back of her head can do wonders to remain calm.

One thing to remember is that at some point, she may feel overstimulated by touch. She may yoyo from needing intense massage on her back to not wanting any physical contact. Stay perceptive to her wants and needs and respond accordingly.

Breathing: The more stressed people are, the shallower and more rapid breathing becomes. This is just a biological response to stress. However, you can reduce stress levels by calming your breathing and taking deliberate deep, slow breaths. With controlled breathing, you're forcing the entire body to relax. Changes in breathing patterns can serve as an indication of contractions starting or ending.

Progressive relaxation:

1. Create a soothing and pleasant environment and guide your partner through visual and meditative techniques.

2. Start at one end of her body—let's say her toes—have her flex and stretch them for a couple of seconds and release them into a relaxed pose.

3. Continue to the feet, ankles, calf muscles, and higher up. Run through every part of the body, first increasing the tension and then letting go into a relaxed state.

4. Couple this with breathing. Hold the tension for as long as she can inhale and hold her breath, and as she relaxes, she can slowly exhale.

This exercise doesn't only bring about a deep sense of relaxation during labor but can be practiced at any place, anywhere, and at any time.

Labor: Throughout the process, you can be sure to rely on the guidance of your doctor or midwife to get you through the process and your baby from your partner's womb and into your arms. For months you've prepared yourself for this moment, but there is still uncertainty about what will happen. Will something go wrong? Try not to focus on the negatives and remain focused on the wonderful occasion. Your baby is ready to exit the womb and become part of your life as an actual little human being you can hold in your arms.

Why Does My Baby Look Like That?

You've waited for this moment for the longest time — the moment when you'll finally meet your baby. You've visualized it, and then, when you see it, the funny appearance of your newborn baby may come as a little bit of a shock.

Skin color: When a baby is born, its skin looks purple or dark red, regardless of its ethnicity. When it starts to breathe, it turns to a brighter red color, and this redness will gradually disappear for a day or two. It may also have a slightly blue tone as its circulation is still improving and getting stronger. Sometimes babies turn yellow. This color change is due to jaundice, which I will expand on shortly.

Vernix: Your baby is covered in a fatty white layer, looking a lot like some type of soft white cheese or Crisco. The layer will be wiped off after delivery, though it was very important, as it protected your baby's skin throughout the pregnancy.

Oddly shaped heads: Your baby may have a weirdly shaped head. Remember that the bones in their skull are still soft and somewhat flexible to ease movement throughout the birth canal. So, when it comes out of the birth canal, these bones might be shaped into an interesting position. It's much the same process as having a fresh loaf of bread at the bottom of your food cart, and when you finally unpack the entire cart and get to the bread, it's shaped, well, strange. Don't worry. Within a week or two, your baby's head will have returned to a normal shape.

Milia: It may initially look like your baby is born with little white pimples on their nose, cheeks, forehead, and chin. But these aren't pimples. Oil glands form these milia, and they'll disappear by themselves. When these white dots appear in your baby's mouth, they are called Epstein pearls.

Stork bites: You may notice on the back of your baby's neck, eyelids, between their eyes, or on the upper lip small red or pink patches. Sticking to the myth that a stork delivers babies, that's how these red marks earned their name. It's actually just a high concentration of immature blood vessels which becomes more evident when your baby is crying. They, too, will fade over time and are usually completely gone when your baby turns 18 months.

Immediately After Birth

What happens to your baby once it's born? As soon as your baby is born, your team of healthcare providers will do some tests to determine that all is well with your little one.

APGAR test: The APGAR test is a routine test given within one minute after birth. The test measures heart rate, breathing by assessing the strength of your baby's crying, muscle tone assessed by looking at how active your baby is, the reflex response by inserting a bulb syringe or something similar into its nose, and the color of your baby's feet, hands, and body. For each of these, your baby will get a score out of 10. After 10 minutes, they'll repeat the test. A score of seven or higher indicates a healthy baby, while a score of four or below may mean your baby will require neonatal care.

Hearing tests: This test usually occurs a while after birth to determine whether your baby can hear. They conduct this test by placing a set of headphones over your baby's ears and sticking electrodes to its head. In the headphones, soft sounds stimulate hearing, which the electrodes measure.

Bilirubin screening: Within 24-36 hours after birth, this test will determine whether your baby has jaundice.

Dried blood spot screening: I cringe thinking about this test, but it's necessary. The test is also called the heel stick test, which is rather self-explanatory. The medical staff will stick a needle into your baby's heel to get drops of blood that needs to be tested for various rare disorders.

Critical congenital heart defect screening: 24 hours after birth, babies can get screened for heart disease to determine if there are any signs or symptoms of heart disease.

Another important thing to remember during this time is skin-on-skin contact which we'll review in more depth in the next chapter.

Potential Complications

Now, we're getting to the most feared subject of the entire process of labor and delivery —complications. Here too, having the necessary knowledge will help you maintain a calmer and more collected approach, enabling you to support your partner who has just been through a huge ordeal to bring your baby to life.

Birth Injuries

A birth injury is precisely what the name states, a physical injury sustained during the birth process. Several factors can contribute to such an injury and increase the likelihood of it occurring. Large babies, maternal obesity, premature births, prolonged labor, your baby being in an unusual position during the birth process, difficult labor, or giving birth while your partner's pelvis isn't of adequate size or shape to get your baby out can all contribute to birth injuries.

Severity and recovery depend on the type of injury sustained.

Brachial palsy: The name is frightening on its own. It refers to damage to the nerves running to the arms and hands and occurs when the baby's shoulder gets stuck during birth. It causes the baby to lose the ability to flex and rotate the arm, but if it's only bruised and swollen, it will recover within a couple of months. If the nerve damage is more severe and perhaps torn, it can be more permanent. Some exercises and therapies, though, can help the healing process.

Bruising or forceps marks: Your baby can sustain bruising to its forehead or face as it travels down the birth canal, bumping into pelvic bones or even tissue. Also, if a forceps or vacuum extraction is used to help with delivery, these apparatuses can leave bruises on your baby's face or head.

Facial paralysis: This is another injury sustained in the birth canal. Your baby may suffer injury to a muscle in the face, causing the loss of facial movement. If it's only nerve damage, it will heal by itself within a couple of weeks, but if the nerve is torn, it will require surgery to fix the concern.

Fractures: The force inside the birth canal can be so severe that your baby can fracture their clavicle or collarbone during a difficult delivery. This, too, will heal quickly and may only need some support to help your baby hold their arm still.

Subconjunctival hemorrhage: There may be damage to the blood vessels in your baby's eye, leaving a visible red band in the eye. The body naturally absorbs this blood, and it will disappear within ten days, leaving no damage to the eye.

When any of the above concerns happen to your baby, it may feel like you don't want to leave its side, but the reality is that healthcare professionals know exactly what they are doing and how to care for your baby. Someone who will need your attention and care is your partner.

These types of incidents can leave your partner with birth trauma. You can and should support her in accessing mental health care. If she is initially unwilling to see such a professional, continue to reassure her that there is help available and that they can help heal from traumatic birth events.

Always refrain from being judgmental and never dismiss the feelings she expresses to you. Acknowledge what has happened and that you under-stand what she is feeling is distressing to her. You are not exempt from these traumas, either! Be sure to recognize and address any mental struggles you may have from the delivery process as well.

Apnea of Prematurity

This is a complex term that basically means your baby has stopped breathing for more than 20 seconds. This can happen in premature and full-term babies, but the more premature the baby, the greater the chances of apnea. It can be caused by bleeding or damage to the brain, infection, acid reflux, heart or blood circulation problems, lung problems, chemical imbalances in the body, or even changes in body temperature. When it happens, your baby may turn bluish while its heart rate slows down. This is due to an oxygen shortage. Witnessing it happen is a scary moment for any parent. However, there are various treatment options to restore parental peace of mind. If your baby has apnea, it will most likely have to stay longer in the hospital, where it can receive proper care to prevent possible long-term lung damage until your medical team clears your baby to go home.

Jaundice

I've touched on this, but let's break it down to the following; your baby breaks down red blood cells into bilirubin. When your baby's liver isn't processing the bilirubin quickly enough, it will start to build up in its tissues and cells. As bilirubin is yellow, it gives your baby a yellow tone to its skin and eyes. Other symptoms are a lack of energy and a poor appetite. This yellow tone can occur within the first 24 hours or a few days after birth. Treatment entails vitamin D drops or phototherapy, meaning your baby is placed under a particular spectrum of lights. This therapy helps the liver to get rid of the excess bilirubin. Another form of phototherapy uses a fiberoptic blanket. In severe cases, your baby may need a blood transfusion. If your baby is breastfeeding, you may also have to supplement the milk with formula, as it can be that your baby isn't receiving enough nutrition.

There are several types of jaundice, each with a unique cause.

- Physiological jaundice results from your baby's inability to get rid of bilirubin.

- Breastfeeding jaundice is linked to the fact that your baby isn't eating enough; therefore, he or she dehydrates and urinates less, causing the bilirubin to build up in its tissues.

- Breast milk jaundice can be caused by a substance in the breast milk preventing proper reabsorption of bilirubin.

- Hemolysis jaundice is linked to Rh disease, causing too many red blood cells in your baby's blood.

- Poor liver function jaundice means your baby's liver doesn't work well.

It's important to remind your partner that there is nothing she can do to prevent this. If the jaundice is linked to breastfeeding, the necessary steps can be taken to stop it from happening. However, even when this is the case, it's still not your partner's fault, and most forms of jaundice can easily be treated.

Stillbirth

The loss of a pregnancy before 20 weeks is called a miscarriage, and thereafter, it's considered a stillbirth. In more than half of the cases, there is no definite cause for this happening. Regardless of whether it's an early, late, or full-term stillbirth, it's a devastating event for any parent. It is emotionally tumultuous, and it will take a huge amount of time to come to terms with what has happened. You and your partner will need both physical and emotional support. It may be necessary to seek professional help together, as this experience can often lead to depression or PTSD. The best thing you can do for yourself and your partner is to remain close and participate in counseling.

FAQs

Q: How common are birth complications?

A: While birth complications can be scary and are every expecting parent's worst nightmare, the statistics indicate that only 8% of all pregnancies involve complications.

Q: How common are fractures during birth?

A: This concern may occur more often than expected. Roughly one out of 11 babies born sustain a fracture during birth. This fracture mostly occurs in the clavicle or collarbone and can even go undetected. However, as your baby's bones are still growing, these fractures heal fairly quickly.

Q: How long does it take for the soft spot on my baby's skull to harden?

A: There are two larger soft spots on your baby's skull. The one at the back is smaller and takes 2-3 months, while the one in front is slightly larger and only closes completely around 18 months.

Journal Prompts

Dealing with any birth complication can be challenging at any level. As the father, you may feel the added pressure of being a comforter, while others may not necessarily see the need to comfort you. This is why it's so important to continue journaling your thoughts and emotions - to ensure healing and recovery and gain the emotional strength to push forward while supporting your partner.

- How will I take care of myself today?

- What boundaries do I need to set to give myself time to recover emotionally?

- List three of your inherent strengths that will help you to make it through this challenging time.

- What areas do I need to seek help in from others?

Conclusion

Why don't eggs tell jokes? They'd crack each other up.

While this chapter may not feel like the time for a joke, It also helps to look at the lighter side of life to make these dark and challenging moments easier to cope with. Meanwhile, being a proactive and loving part of everything will help you bond with your wife and baby. In the next step of the journey, we'll explore what happens when you bring your little one and beautiful partner home.

Chapter 11

A Whole New World at Home

I don't know who you'll be, but I know you'll be my everything.
—Anonymous

Congratulations on your precious and magnificent new family member (or members). The time has come to bring your baby home. So, you'll need to know everything about ensuring you, your partner, and your baby are well, safe, and happy. Bringing your partner and baby home is such an accomplishment and a proud moment. You're a dad, and it's time to become an expert father. You're still advocating for your partner, but your baby needs you, too. You can do this! In this final chapter, you will find empowerment in having an understanding of the journey ahead while making the most of your role as a caring dad and loving partner.

Bringing Your Baby Home

When will you be able to bring your baby home? If your baby is born from a healthy pregnancy at full term, you'll most likely be able to take him or her home within 24-48 hours after birth. Even a preterm baby born between weeks 34 and 36 might be discharged from the hospital in just over 48 hours. If you had to undergo a C-section or there were other complications, it might take a little longer before getting the green light to go home, while babies born younger than 34 weeks may have an even longer stay to ensure they are strong enough. In a sense, it also gives you and your partner time to adapt to the idea of looking after such a small person without having a team of medical experts on standby.

Maybe everything you needed was packed in the hospital bag, or perhaps your partner sent you home to straighten the house and grab some things she'd like before leaving the hospital with your newborn. She will likely opt for comfortable and loose-fitting clothes for the trip home. It's often the case that babies get completely overdressed on the day they go home for the first time. Ditch the designer outfit and dress them in something that will go on without the struggle of upsetting your little one.

The Car Trip

Being the brilliant hen you're inspired to be, the car seat—complying with safety standards, has been fitted, likely checked by the discharge nurse, and awaits your baby. This will be the only seat where your baby is safe in the car. Please, don't ever convince yourself that it's okay to hold your baby on your lap, even if you have a distraught newborn. The majority of accidents occur within a short distance of your home, and even if it's a low-speed accident, it can still cause enough force to injure your baby or cause them to be flung from your arms. Experts in the field have invested years of research and development to design the safest seat for your baby. You have to spend a lot of money buying it. So, use it and use it correctly. Be sure you've read the manufacturer's guidelines so your baby is buckled in safely.

Something you might not have expected is that you may have mixed emotions when you step out of that hospital or birthing center. Sure, there is a lot of excitement, but a bit of nervousness also surfaces and gets the better of you from time to time. This is totally normal. While you may have been expecting and looking forward to this moment, there is no way to be completely prepared for what it will be like. You just don't know—especially with your first baby. If you already have other kids waiting at home, the moment can also be challenging as now you need to attend to your baby's needs and those of your other children. All while being a supportive partner and dealing with your own emotions. You must understand how important self-care is for dads to thrive and reach their full potential in fatherhood.

It's a good idea to set boundaries and limit visitors during the first couple of days in order to not overwhelm your baby or your partner. It's hard to find your feet during the first couple of days without the support of the hospital staff, and you need to establish a routine at home.

Realizing that you no longer have the support of a medical team may leave you fretting about when to call a doctor. You know there is a delicate balance between being an alert parent and a paranoid parent, and finding that line can be tricky at the start. As a tip to all first-time parents out there, concerns that justify calling a doctor during the first couple of days are as follows.

- If the soft spot on their head bulges when they're held upright

- If they vomit forcefully and can't hold any fluids down

- If there is blood in their vomit or stool

- If they have diarrhea for more than eight hours

- If they start to show symptoms of dehydration

- If they develop a fever – for babies, this is 100.4°F rectal temperature

Handling Your Baby

In addition to caring for their health needs, handling this tiny person is another overwhelming idea to overcome. As men, we're not always that gentle, and maybe you're scared of hurting your baby. I felt extremely awkward and uneasy each time I held one of our newborns. Their tiny light frames and their floppy heads are intimidating to cradle. By sticking to the following four tips, you can easily overcome this mental challenge.

Always keep one hand underneath your baby's head and neck. Their necks aren't strong enough to carry their heads yet, and the lack of support can cause injury.

Always wash your hands before touching your baby. Their immune systems may have the necessary building block in place, but it will be another couple of years before they're fully developed and strong enough to fend off most germs, so don't be the cause of premature exposure.

Always strap your baby in, whether it's in a car seat, stroller, or carrier. They might not be mobile, but one wrong move and they can slide right out, causing injury.

Never shake your baby. Not even if they won't stop crying and you're tired and frustrated. I know your first thought was, "Who will ever do something like that?" Let me tell you now that there might come days—my heart's wish for you is that this doesn't happen—when you're so tired and have tried so many things to get your baby to stop crying, and it just doesn't... and you don't know what to do to make it stop... and frustration kicks in and shaking can happen. Take a breather and call in for support. Ask a family member or friend to come and help so that you and your partner can get the rest you need. Shaking a baby can have such severe repercussions - your baby can die.

Bonding

Bonding with your child now is as important as it will be for the rest of your life. The way you bond with your child will only vary as they age. The best way to bond with your tiny baby is through skin-on-skin contact. Avoid any strong deodorant or cologne, and find a quiet spot where you and the baby can sit comfortably without a shirt and your baby only in its diaper. This will mean a room with dim lighting and a pleasant temperature. Now, hold your baby on your chest and just talk in a soft, soothing voice. Sing, hum, or tell a story to your little one. It doesn't matter. It's about your baby feeling your skin, creating a bond, and letting your baby hear your voice. Bonding in this way will boost your confidence as a father and create a sense of protectiveness, but you and your baby will also both benefit from it. Some of these benefits are:

- Research indicates that a baby's brain development speeds up when there are a lot of skin-on-skin contact sessions (*Benefits of Skin-To-Skin Contact between Dad & Baby*, 2015).

- It's a great stress relief for you both, but especially for your baby.

- They sleep much better.

- Their immune system improves as you pass antibodies to them through skin-on-skin contact.

- A baby is likely to pick up weight faster.

- After a while, your breathing and heartbeat synchronize, helping your baby.

Swaddling

Initially, swaddling may seem like an art you'll never be able to master, but it isn't that hard once you get it right.

1. Spread out your baby's blanket and then fold back one corner slightly.

2. Lay your baby down on the blanket facing upwards with its head slightly above the corner you've folded over.

3. Fold the left corner over your baby and tuck it in underneath its right arm.

4. Bring the bottom corner up towards your baby's face.

5. Bring the right corner around your baby.

6. If the blanket is high up, you may have to push it down to allow for easy breathing and be sure that it isn't too tight around their legs, allowing some space for movement.

By swaddling your baby like this, you give them the feeling of being in their mother's womb, a place of safety. However, this will only work until they're about two months old, and then they may start to roll over, and swaddling is no longer a feasible option.

Feeding Time

How do you know your baby is hungry? They'll tell you by crying, making sucking noises, or putting their hands in their mouths.

You'll know your baby is a happy and satisfied eater when they gain weight, sleep well after being fed, look happy and content, and have roughly six wet diapers and a couple of daily poops.

What to Expect the First Few Days

Up until now, you've studied all the material you could lay your hands on, read every book you could find—or your partner found for you to read—and might even have watched a bunch of YouTube videos, but now your practical exam is here and failing isn't an option.

No worries, I've got you. You need to know the following things about newborns.

Babies need to be burped. This might be the only time in their lives when you'll see expressions of elation and gratitude after the sound of a burp. Not long from now, it will be frowned upon for life. While some babies are capable of doing it on their own, most babies need to be burped. This entails gently patting their backs in a circular motion to bring up any air that was swallowed during feeding so that it doesn't cause them pain and discomfort. You can hold your baby upright on your lap, let them lie with their head on your shoulder, or they can even sit supported on your knee, leaning forward with one hand holding the head under the chin. When you do this, they may spit or even hiccup, which is completely normal. Excessive fussing can occur when they are experiencing gas issues. Be sure to spend extra time burping to eliminate discomfort and also practice bicycle kicks. This is where you hold their legs and pedal them back and forth, each time lightly pressing their knee into their belly. This may feel awkward at first, but you won't be hurting them; in fact, it's an excellent way to help them relieve gas in their tummy.

If your baby is crying when they spit up or is arching its back, it may have reflux, which is similar to heartburn. Flashback to the time you had one too many hot dogs at that barbeque; you can understand your baby's unhappiness and discomfort. Keep them upright and always have a burp cloth nearby to wipe away the spit-up.

Normal bowel movements for your baby will be a couple of dirty diapers and roughly ten wet diapers daily. Breastfed babies tend to poop more often than those who drink formula. Keep track of your baby's bowel movements. Having this record will make it evident if there are any changes and will give you a more accurate explanation of your baby's health when visiting the pediatrician. Although breastfed babies can have more bowel movements than formula-fed babies, the opposite can also be true. Our youngest actually went 17 days without a dirty diaper other than wet ones. As you can imagine, this was alarming to us even after only 48 hours. After many calls and a visit to the pediatrician over the next few weeks, she reassured us that we had a very healthy baby. There were no other health concerns, and our doctor explained that infants can process breastmilk extremely well, sometimes resulting in no bowel movements. The longest one of her infant patients went without a bowel movement was 27 days! This would certainly worry any parent, so never feel too sheepish to contact your pediatrician with any concerns at all.

Diaper changing should never be only one parent's responsibility, and saying that you don't know how to do it, is no excuse. If you don't know, learn! Practicing this stinky skill will help the two of you share the load of baby-care (pun intended). Once you've done it several times, you'll know it isn't that hard.

Newborn babies sleep for roughly 16 hours during the 24-hour cycle. They do this in 2-4 hour stretches. As your baby grows older, it will develop its own unique sleep pattern. Place your baby on its back to sleep and Avoid using blankets, stuffed animals, and crib bumpers to reduce the risk of sudden infant death syndrome (SIDS). SIDS is the sudden death of an infant due to unexplained causes and occurs most frequently in infants two to four months old. Use a thin swaddle or sleep sack instead of blankets. While it may be convenient, avoid sharing your bed with your baby for the same reason.

Newborn babies cry. However, initially, your newborn may sleep more than cry, but once babies grow older, they can start to cry more often and for longer periods. If your baby cries a lot—like for three hours without end —it can be due to digestive issues or colic, and it's best to see your doctor about it.

Remember that crying is your baby's only way of communicating, and the longer you spend time together, the better you'll be at figuring out what your baby needs to soothe the crying.

Newborn breathing is something that can also freak parents out. At times your baby may be breathing quickly and then stop for a few seconds. These can be the longest seconds in your life, but it's normal. When should you call a doctor? When your baby is grunting, its nostrils flare, breathing remains consistently fast, there are wheezing sounds coming from its chest, its lips have lost color or are blue, or there are pauses of 10-15 seconds between breaths.

For the first couple of days, there is no need to bathe your baby. Its umbilical cord is still a delicate stump until it fulls scabs and falls off by itself after a few days. You can only clean your baby with a warm wet cloth or sponge. You should give your baby a regular wipe to clean up spilled milk or spit up around the face and the folds around the neck. Your newborn's skin may also be looking a little odd. During the first couple of days or weeks, cradle cap (dead skin build up on the scalp), newborn rash, and dryness are common. Don't stress about this - it can sometimes take a while for your baby's skin to regulate and get used to life outside the womb. Your baby will soon have that smooth skin you expect a newborn to have.

While on the topic of the umbilical cord—during birth, this is cut, and the stump is left on your baby. Over the next couple of days, it will dry up until it falls off. Don't ever pull on it, and be sure to wash around it with care. If it does ever show any signs of redness, has a foul smell, is swelling, or has yellow fluid draining from it, call your doctor. These can be signs of infection.

You or your partner might be tempted to dress your baby in all those trendy outfits you've been stocking, but during the newborn stage, it's so much easier to go for simple items that are easy to change. Also, rely on your common sense to determine how warm you need to dress your baby. Remember that your baby is likely to be slightly colder than you. A rule of thumb could be to dress them in similar clothes to the ones you are wearing, plus one layer or a thin blanket. Just watch your baby to see if it's too warm after a while.

While you've stocked up on all the nifty baby gear you need, you will likely not use all of them right at the moment. For now, you only need a baby wrap, sling, or carrier, and of course, a properly installed car seat.

Who doesn't like a good massage? Your baby sure enjoys one. Remember that their bodies also get sore from all the lying and being carried around. At times, they may feel uncomfortable while being held or laid down and can't change their position themselves—or say, "Hey! Move me!" So, it is well worth your time to study baby massaging techniques and practice them with your baby. Even when they are still so small, it's a wonderful way to get your baby to relax and fall asleep. Always use clean hands and warm them up before touching your baby. This can be another great bonding activity.

To a certain extent, massaging is also a form of skin-on-skin contact. Remember that this type of contact isn't limited to your stay in the hospital. You can continue doing this regularly at home to strengthen your connection.

The best advice on all these matters remains to trust your gut - doing so will give you confidence that you really are developing fatherly instincts. You know your baby better than anyone else, and if something feels right or doesn't, even if you can't quite put a finger on it, go with your gut.

Breastfeeding

There are a couple of things you can learn about breastfeeding too. During the first few days, your partner will only be producing colostrum. This nutrient-dense milk is high in antioxidants and antibodies and helps to build your baby's immune system. Colostrum is low in fat and sugar but high in protein. Your baby only needs a little bit of this thicker milk with a yellow tone. After about two to four days, it will turn into transitional milk. The stage of transitional milk lasts for about two weeks, and only then your partner's body will start to produce mature milk, which will be the case until her body is done producing milk, either by itself or when she starts to wean your baby off breastfeeding.

When should you feed your baby? There are several approaches you can follow. Some parents like to schedule certain feeding times, while others opt for responsive feeding. This means you watch your baby closely and get to know its behavior and patterns. It's how you'll see when your baby is hungry before it starts crying. Preferably, you don't want your baby to cry if you can prevent it, as crying releases stress hormones. This close observation of your baby is another way to strengthen your bond. Cues to look out for are rooting, waving, wriggling, moving its eyes, sucking its fist, or making murmuring noises.

Responsive breastfeeding is good for your partner and your baby. For your baby, it means getting all the milk it needs to grow stronger and stay healthy at the times its body needs it, and for your partner, it means that her breasts don't get too full and inflamed but that there also is enough time to produce sufficient milk to feed your baby. Your partner needs two or perhaps more breastfeeding bras, a breast pump if necessary, and plenty of vitamin D to support her on this journey. However, it may be something she might initially struggle with since it can be hard to get your baby in the correct position for optimal breastfeeding. Breastfeeding can take a lot of practice for both your partner and baby. You may notice your partner getting into odd positions to accommodate a better latch. However, it's important that she is comfortable. Helping her to prop up her arms for support and elevating her feet can aid in a good breastfeeding experience. This will help her to feel more relaxed and to hold the baby close. Also, having a pillow underneath your baby to lift it closer to the breast will help, as well as holding them on their sides to face the breast.

The first several times, your baby may struggle to latch. This can be very frustrating, especially to your partner, as her breasts are getting fuller, your baby is getting hungrier, is crying, and it just doesn't want to take the nipple. She can encourage your baby to latch by brushing its lips against her nipple. Once it opens its mouth, tilt its head back a little and draw the baby nearer to the breast. The nipple and the area below it must go into your baby's mouth so that the nipple is pointing up against the roof of its mouth. Once it feels comfortable, the latch is usually successful.

One challenge a lot of breastfeeding moms face is sore nipples. This can be caused by your baby's feeding position or not being latched properly. It will also help to wear a cotton bra and to let a few drops of breastmilk dry on the nipple. Another helpful aid is purified lanolin. Rub a small amount of lanolin cream on the nipple to ease the pain, but if it isn't getting better, it's best to get professional advice. Extremely sore, inflamed, or red nipples can indicate mastitis - an infection within the milk ducts of the breast. Symptoms include swelling, tenderness, redness, and fever. Treatment for mastitis includes massage, warm compress, continued breastfeeding from the infected side, and usually antibiotics.

Breast pumps are helpful to get enough milk on hand to give your partner a break to rest and for self-care. We've already explored the differences between breast pumps and manual pumps. Always read the manufacturer's manual to be sure you're using it correctly. If you don't have a pump yet, most insurance companies in the US cover the purchase. Check your coverage and see if you can order one.

Always use proper storing techniques to be sure the milk is safe for your baby. Use food-grade containers of glass or BPA-free plastic with tight lids. Never leave milk for longer than four days in the refrigerator. If frozen, you can keep it for up to six months. At room temperature, milk is only good for four hours.

Recovery after birth can be a lengthy process that can take a couple of weeks. Initially, your partner will still have vaginal bleeding while she'll likely also experience abdominal pain due to the uterus contracting to its original size. This may worsen when she is breastfeeding - something that will also increase the amount of bleeding. Dani described her contraction pain with breastfeeding as similar to delivery pain. Do what you can to aid the breastfeeding process, whether that be to help hold the baby off of her sensitive tummy or quickly whisk the baby away to burp them while she breathes through the discomfort of contractions. Vaginal birth can also lead to hemorrhoids causing swelling and pain in the rectum. She will also have vaginal pain due to possible tearing or an episiotomy during labor. Hormonal shifts are inevitable, often causing baby blues. Add to that sore nipples, tender breasts, cramps with breastfeeding, plus sleep deprivation, and you can't help but feel sorry for her and want to give her a medal for bravery.

Recovery from a C-section is somewhat different and will take longer than recovery from vaginal birth. Your partner will also have to rely much more on you if this is the position you're finding yourselves in. She may still experience vaginal bleeding for up to six weeks after giving birth. This specific discharge, called lochia, will turn pink and then yellow and on to white before disappearing. Her wound will initially be pink and raised and may look a bit puffy. That is normal. You should be concerned, though, if she is experiencing excessive pain for more than three days. Tenderness in the area can last up to three weeks, but gradually, this scar will become thinner and less obvious. She will appreciate help getting to her 4-6 week checkups.

You can help her clean her dressing once daily. Showering if the wound was closed with staples, glue, or stitches is also perfectly fine, but it's best to avoid soaking in a bath right now. The doctor will ask her to call if she is bleeding heavily after more than four days, has light bleeding for more than four weeks, or is passing blood clots. Other concerning signs are swelling in one of her legs, redness, swelling, drainage from the wound or if it seems to be opening up, pain in her belly, fever, or if her vaginal discharge has an odor.

Recovery is hard, and your partner will benefit from your emotional support, daily encouragement, and positive affirmations. Here are some examples to use, but also create your own.

- You are the best mother for our baby.

- Today is a new and exciting day for our family.

- Yes, there are challenges, but our baby feels loved and safe.

- I believe in you.

- You are so much more than enough.

- You can handle all the daily struggles.

- I am so proud of you.

- It's okay to have a bad day. This will pass.

- We learn as we go.

- We learn and become better parents every day.

Postpartum Depression

You know, as I recount all the physical challenges the mother goes through during pregnancy, after birth, and the level of exhaustion both of you have, it becomes much more evident why so many new parents struggle with this type of depression. Becoming parents can be physically, mentally, emotionally, and financially daunting.

Recovering from baby blues can happen relatively quickly, but postpartum depression is a much more serious concern. It was a challenge we faced as Dani's mental health took a turn for the worse after having our third child. Postpartum depression affects the lives of roughly one out of every seven women, so it's quite common. Even so, it's a concern that often goes undiagnosed; hence, the number is likely to be even higher. With Dani struggling with this type of depression and witnessing my wife going through this challenge, it taught me many things, but the most important lesson I want to convey is that it can happen to anyone. Ignore any preconceived stigmas or worries of judgment. This situation is, unfortunately, common, but you have many people to turn to for support.

Postpartum depression can be divided into three categories:

Baby blues: An emotional state affecting the lives of about 60-80% of all mothers after delivering a baby (Cleveland Clinic, 2022). It entails bouts of crying without any reason. Your partner is likely feeling increased anxiety and sadness. The crying typically starts within four days after delivery and subsides within a couple of weeks.

Postpartum depression: This is a much more serious concern, and if it was present after a previous pregnancy, your partner is far more likely to have it again. You can expect bouts of emotional highs and lows coupled with increased irritability, fatigue, and crying. This, too, starts within a couple of days to maybe a week after delivery but can last up to a year. However, there is no need to have your partner suffer like this, as plenty of treatment options will bring your partner the relief she needs.

Symptoms to be aware of are

- A loss of appetite.

- Loss of energy

- Losing interest in things your partner used to enjoy

- Being overwhelmed by feelings of hopelessness, sadness, or guilt

- Excessive crying

Postpartum psychosis: This is the most severe diagnosis on the spectrum of postpartum depression and calls for immediate medical intervention. It will present itself shortly after delivery, but the good news is that it's a rare mental health concern and only affects the lives of about 1 out of every 1,000 women. It's a mental health concern that poses the risk of suicide or even harming your baby (Cleveland Clinic, 2022).

In addition to the postpartum depression symptoms, symptoms unique to postpartum psychosis include

- Excessive worrying

- Struggling to focus

- Suicidal thoughts

If any of these symptoms appear in your home, it's best to immediately reach out to your healthcare provider, midwife, doula, or mental health expert.

It's vital to support your partner and remind her that how she feels is not her fault. Research indicates that postpartum depression is likely caused by a rapid drop in hormone levels after delivery (Cleveland Clinic, 2022). Coupled with chemical changes in the body, the lack of sleep, and the changes in your relationship, your partner may find herself in the middle of an emotional storm she can't control.

Is this a concern that can affect your baby? Unfortunately, yes, it can. Your partner's depression can impact her ability to connect with your baby. The short-term consequences can be a poor eating or sleeping routine for your baby, or in extreme cases your baby may be neglected. Long-term consequences are learning disorders, poor social skills, and even concerns like obesity or developmental disorders at a later stage in life.

What can you do to help her? Jump in and lighten her load by doing more things around the house. Be the gatekeeper to ensure she has a safe space to recover in private. List your concerns and address them with your doctor, go with her to doctor's appointments, and learn as much as possible about her condition. The most important thing to do, though, is to be with her. Sometimes all she may need is to have you sitting next to her. Don't talk, don't try to fix her, tell her to get over it or that it's just a phase. Do not tell her that you liked her more before delivery, that she is just tired, or that it's part of becoming a mom. No! Just be there, attentive, dependable, and still.

If there are any life-changing or heavy decisions the two of you need to make, postpone them if possible. Wait until she feels up to it. You can encourage her to do certain things or to engage with others who will lift her spirits, but don't force her if she isn't up to it. Be the comfort and confidant she needs.

Now, while this is a challenging time for mothers, don't underestimate the importance of taking care of your emotional and mental health too. In chapter two, we discussed how high the rate of postpartum depression is in dads, and you have to access the necessary support, take time out, and give yourself the care you need, too, to be sure that you're taking care of yourself.

Secret Dad Tip

Tip #10:

Be the gatekeeper: If there is one position you, as the dad to a newborn, can easily fulfill, then it's that of a gatekeeper. You're biologically built to be a great father. You have millions of years of evolution on your side. Trust your instincts. No matter what anyone says, it's all worth it. So, be your greatest self and take charge. One thing new parents overlook is slowly allowing the family to come to see the baby. Your partner may be emotionally overwhelmed and physically drained. In addition, you're physically exhausted and mentally drained, so limit the number of people coming by in the first weeks. Be sure they're healthy, and don't feel bad asking them not to come around if they're feeling sick. Your baby's immune system is still getting stronger, and while an aunt's runny nose will be long forgotten, you may still have to deal with an unhappy, uncomfortable, and sick baby. It's also perfectly okay to ask them to wash their hands before touching your baby.

Take photos and videos because they'll last longer than the exhausted memories of a newborn. In addition, they'll capture the cutest moments with your family. Get a phone with a fantastic camera - it's worth the investment with your growing family—and snap everything imaginable. This time passes quickly, so make it count.

You can also be the one who slowly introduces your newborn to any family pets. First, let your pets greet your partner to get familiar with the new smells, and then gradually show your pet the baby. Do this calmly, not to excite your pets too much, and ensure you remain in charge of the situation.

FAQs

Q: Will our baby recognize our smell?

A: Newborn babies have a very well-developed sense of smell and can recognize the smells of their parents. Therefore it's best to lay off a heavy deodorant.

Q: I heard their stool is a weird color. Is that true?

A: Yes! It looks weird, but it's normal. Initially, the stool is blackish-green, and then it turns mustard yellow. This happens when your baby is breast-fed, and your partner's milk changes from colostrum to mature milk. If your baby is formula-fed, the stool is larger and less regular and has a tannish color.

Q: How do I change a diaper?

A: Start by getting all you need together in one place and within reach. Lay your baby on its back on the changing table and remove the old diaper. Wipe your baby from the front to the back using baby wipes. Apply diaper cream to treat or prevent diaper rash. Put on the new diaper, place your baby in a safe place where it can't roll over and fall, and wash your hands. Never leave your baby unattended while changing a diaper.

Checklist

There are so many things you may want to think of to get and do when you bring your baby home. However, if these long lists leave you feeling more overwhelmed and even instill an urge to procrastinate, it may be better to draft a short checklist of the essentials. In addition to being a loving mom and dad, here is a short list of must-haves.

- An approved car seat is correctly installed.

- An appropriate place to sleep.

- The necessary tools to feed your baby.

- Diapers—enough in various sizes.

- Clothing and blankets for your baby.

- Bathing supplies, or what you'll need to give your baby a proper wipe during the first couple of days.

- Medical supplies you may need during the first couple of days.

See? This isn't so bad after all.

Conclusion

What did the slow tomato say to the others? Don't worry; I'll ketchup.

Right now, you might be feeling like a slow tomato, wondering if you'll ever feel like a do-it-all super dad. Some moments make you doubt yourself or feel different about your partner. It's normal to feel offbeat in the first few weeks. Both of you became parents, which is monumentally successful and stressful. Meanwhile, choose to slow down, take a breath and revel in the beauty of the family you two have created.

Conclusion

Never is a man more of a man than when he is a father of a newborn. —Matthew McConaughey

Capturing the details and changes that took place in Dani's body with each of our three children reminds me of how much I admire her physical, mental, and emotional strength. If the birthing process fell on men, I think we would've been lucky to have had one child. Women are strong in ways we, as men, don't understand, yet they still need love and support from their partners.

As a dad, feeling close to your baby during pregnancy and sometimes even after birth can be hard. The way to overcome this distance is to offer constant support and familiarize yourself with every aspect of the pregnancy. Gain as much knowledge as possible to make informed decisions and know exactly what to expect, how to approach challenges, and how to be the best teammate you can be to your partner.

While it's important to look after your partner and unborn child, soon to be your family, you can only do so by giving them your best and taking care of yourself too. It's why this book puts a lot of emphasis on self-care.

Now that you're a parent, you will rely on your instincts more than ever before in your life. While I'm no doctor or expert when it comes to either emotional or physical wellness, I hope you were able to glean some nuggets of wisdom from the experiences I've accumulated and shared by being the hen during three pregnancies. While you may have to adapt my suggestions to suit your unique situation better, I can say with certainty the things I've shared are the things that worked for me, my partner, and our family.

Knowledge can remove the terrible insecurities within you. Applying this wisdom will open your world, mind, and fatherly desires to a new realm.

Pregnancy and delivery can be a rollercoaster of challenges for both of you, but the reward, the love of a family, and the bond that exists in our home are something I would never swap for anything.

My wife and I wish you the best on your journey!

Hey there, New Father!

We hope you've enjoyed this book and found it entertaining, informative, and valuable as you prepared for your new arrival.

It's your support and feedback that help us in our quest to provide quality resources for expectant fathers like you... Please take 60 seconds to help other new fathers and kindly leave a review on Amazon!

Here's how:

1. **Scan QR code** with your phone's camera

2. **Scroll down & click** "Write a customer review"

Web Link: (*U.S. readers only*) https://www.amazon.com/review/create-review/?asin=B0CMFGKT79

Embrace your new adventure and enjoy every second because it passes way too fast! From the bottom of our hearts,

THANK YOU for your support!

References

Aggarwal, N. (2022, June 13). *20 Positive parenting affirmations to boost your mental health*. The Bump. https://www.thebump.com /a/positive-parenting-affirmations

Amniocentesis. (2022, January 4). Cleveland Clinic. https://my.clevelandclinic.org/health/treatments/4206-genetic-amni ocentesis#:~:text=What%20does%20amniocentesis

Amniotic fluid problems/hydramnios/oligohydramnios. (n.d.). The Children's Hospital of Philadelphia. https://www.chop.edu/conditions-diseases/amniotic-fluid-problemshydr amniosoligohydramnios#:~:text=What%20are%20the%20symptoms%20 of%20hydramnios

Apnea of prematurity . (n.d.). University Hospitals. https://www.uhhospitals.org/rainbow/services/pediatric-neonatology/co nditions-and-treatments/article/Diseases-and-Conditions---Pediatrics/ap nea-of-prematurity#:~:text=Apnea%20of%20Prematurity

Baby movements in pregnancy. (n.d.). Tommys. https://www.tommys.org/pregnancy-information/pregnancy-sym ptom-checker/baby-fetal-movements#:~:text=How%20often%20should

Barry, J. (2020, November 17). *10 Pregnancy conversations you need to have with your partner.* Kidspot. https://www.kidspot.com.au/birth/pregnancy/pregnancy-health/10-pre

gnancy-conversations-you-need-to-have-with-your-partner/news-story/8
07303d96f318a8cb5e42086b5abbda6

Beginners   guide   to   breastfeeding.   (n.d.).   Emma's   Diary. https://www.emmasdiary.co.uk/baby/breastfeeding/beginners-guid
e-to-breastfeeding#:~:text=RESPONSIVE%20FEEDING

BellyBelly.   (2022,   July   29).   *15   Great   ways
to   support   her   during   pregnancy*.   BellyBelly. https://www.bellybelly.com.au/men/15-great-ways-to-support-your
-partner-during-pregnancy/#:~:text=%231%3A%20Help%20without

Benefits of skin-to-skin contact between dad & baby. (2015, June 21).
NuRoo. https://nuroobaby.com/skin-to-skin/the-benefits-of-skin-to-sk
in-contact-between-dad-baby/

Ben-Joseph, E. P. (2023, May). *A guide for first-time parents*. Kids Health.
https://kidshealth.org/en/parents/guide-parents.html

Birth   injuries.   (n.d.).   University   Hospitals.
https://www.uhhospitals.org/rainbow/services/pediatric-neonatology/co
nditions-and-treatments/article/Pediatric-Diseases-and-Conditions-v0/b
irth-injuries#:~:text=What%20is%20a

Boyle,   A.   (2013,   June   15).   *This   is   your   brain   on   fatherhood: Dads experience hormonal changes too, research shows*. NBC
News. https://www.nbcnews.com/sciencemain/your-brain-fatherhood
-dads-experience-hormonal-changes-too-research-shows-6C10333109

Bradley, S. (2020, January 21). *Can sex in the first trimester cause miscarriage? Early pregnancy sex questions*. Healthline. https://www.healthline
.com/health/pregnancy/sex-first-12-weeks-of-pregnancy#pain

Breech baby. (n.d.). Cleveland Clinic. https://my.clevelandclinic.org/hea
lth/diseases/21848-breech-baby#:~:text=How%20does%20a

Bringing your baby home. (2018, June). Kids Health. https://kidshea lth.org/en/parents/bringing-baby-home.html

Burker, V. (2021, October 18). *6 Ways to show up for the preeclampsia mom in your life*. Preeclampsia Foundation . https://www.preeclampsia.org/the-news/community-support/6-way s-to-show-up-for-the-preeclampsia-mom-in-your-life#:~:text=How% 20to%20Show%20Up%20for%20a%20Preeclampsia%20Mom

C-Section . (n.d.). Cleveland Clin- ic. https://my.clevelandclinic.org/health/treatments/7246-cesarean -birth-c-section#:~:text=What%20is%20a

Calantuoni, F., & Rajbhandari, S. (2021, March 5). *A fresh look at paternity leave: Why the benefits extend beyond the personal*. Mckinsey & Company. https://www.mckinsey.com/capabilities/people-and-organizational-p erformance/our-insights/a-fresh-look-at-paternity-leave-why-the-ben efits-extend-beyond-the-personal

Carroll, M. C. (2022, August 10). *These are the funniest dad jokes, according to kids*. Parents. https://www.parents.com/fun/funniest-d ad-jokes-for-kids/#:~:text=What%20do%20you

CDC. (2022a, June 16). *Diagnosis of birth defects*. Centers for Disease Control and Prevention. https://www.cdc.gov/ncbddd/birthdefects /diagnosis.html#:~:text=First%20Trimester%20Screening

CDC. (2022b, December 30). *Awareness of birth defects across the lifespan* . Centers for Disease Control and Preven- tion. https://www.cdc.gov/ncbddd/birthdefects/features/birth-defe cts-awareness.html#:~:text=adolescence%2C%20and%20adulthood.-

Certified nurse midwife. (n.d.). Top Nursing. https://www.topnursi ng.org/career/certified-nurse-midwife/

Cleveland Clinic. (2022, April 12). *Postpartum depression*. Cleveland Clinic Medical Professional. https://my.clevelandclinic.org/health/diseases/9312-postpartum-depression

Cleveland Clinic Medical Professional. (2020, August 27). *Stillbirth*. Cleveland Clinic. https://my.clevelandclinic.org/health/diseases/9685-stillbirth#:~:text=What%20can%20I

Cleveland Clinic Medical Professional. (2022, February 21). *Colostrum*. Cleveland Clinic. https://my.clevelandclinic.org/health/body/22434-colostrum#:~:text=Colostrum

Complications of pregnancy. (n.d.). Hopkins Medicine. https://www.hopkinsmedicine.org/health/conditions-and-diseases/staying-healthy-during-pregnancy/complications-of-pregnancy#:~:text=Amniotic%20fluid%20complications

Do I need to go to the hospital when my water breaks? (n.d.). Maryland State Doulas. https://www.marylandstatedoulas.com/blog/do-i-need-to-go-to-the-hospital-when-my-water-breaks#:~:text=Do%20you%20need

Edelstein, R. S., Chopik, W. J., Saxbe, D. E., Wardecker, B. M., Moors, A. C., & LaBelle, O. P. (2016). Prospective and dyadic associations between expectant parents' prenatal hormone changes and postpartum parenting outcomes. *Developmental Psychobiology*, *59*(1), 77–90. https://doi.org/10.1002/dev.21469

Epidurals. (n.d.). Made for This Moment. https://www.asahq.org/madeforthismoment/pain-management/techniques/epidural/#:~:text=needle%20is%20inserted.-

Epidurals: Need it or leave it? (n.d.). Walnut Hill OBGYN. https://walnuthillobgyn.com/blog/epidurals-need-it-or-leave-it/#:~:text=Is%20an%20epidural%20right

Episiotomy.   (n.d.).   Hopkins   Medicine. https://www.hopkinsmedicine.org/health/treatment-tests-and
-therapies/episiotomy#:~:text=What%20is%20an

Exercise during pregnancy. (n.d.). March of Dimes.
https://www.marchofdimes.org/find-support/topics/pregnancy/exer
cise-during-pregnancy#:~:text=How%20much%20exercise%20do%20
you

Feuerman, M. (2022, June 25). *Saving your relationship when you
disagree on parenting.* Verywell Family. https://www.verywellfamily.c
om/tips-dont-agree-on-parenting-4107372#:~:text=It%20is%20not

First   trimester   fatigue .   (n.d.).   University
of   Rochester   Medical   Center   Health   Encyclope-
dia. https://www.urmc.rochester.edu/encyclopedia/content.aspx?co
ntenttypeid=134&contentid=4#:~:text=What%20causes%20the

First week at home with your newborn baby . (n.d.). Baby Center. https://www.babycenter.com/baby/newborn-baby/newborn-ba
by_10345806

4 Common pregnancy complications. (2022, October 18). Hopkins
M   e   d   i   c   i   n   e   .
https://www.hopkinsmedicine.org/health/conditions-and-diseases/st
aying-healthy-during-pregnancy/4-common-pregnancy-complication
s#:~:text=You%20might%20be%20as%20excited

Gamble, L. (2022, May 18). *12 conversations to have with your partner
before your baby arrives.* Tell Me Baby. https://tellmebaby.com.au/pr
egnancy/12-conversations-with-partner-before-birth/

Gestational   Hypertension.   (n.d.).   Stanford   Medicine. https://www.stanfordchildrens.org/en/topic/default?id=gestat
ional-hypertension-90-P02484#:~:text=What%20are%20the

Giving   birth   to   multiple   babies .   (n.d.).   Tommys. https://www.tommys.org/pregnancy-information/giving-birth /giving-birth-multiple-babies#:~:text=Where%20will%20I

Glossary - Pregnancy and Childbirth. (n.d.). Stanford Children. https://www.stanfordchildrens.org/en/topic/default?id=gloss ary---pregnancy-and-childbirth-85-P01219

Going home after a C-section information. (n.d.). Mount Sinai Health S   y   s   t   e   m   . https://www.mountsinai.org/health-library/discharge-instructions/g oing-home-after-a-c-section#:~:text=What%20to%20Expect%20at

Gordon, K. (2019, October 8). *Your ultimate dad-to-be cheat sheet.* Parents. https://www.parents.com/parenting/dads/101/ultimate-da d-to-be-checklist/

Guide for first-time parents. (2018). Kids Health. https://kidshealth. org/en/parents/guide-parents.html

Happity. (n.d.). *15 unexpected facts you may learn as a new dad.* Happity   Blog. https://www.happity.co.uk/blog/article/15-unexpected-facts-you-ma y-learn-as-a-new-dad/#7-if-you-are-a-new-dad-you-can-experience-pn d:~:text=hold%20of%20it.-

Health Direct Australia. (2021, September). *Making a birth plan.* Pregnancy Birth Baby. https://www.pregnancybirthbaby.org.au/mak ing-a-birth-plan#:~:text=your%20original%20plan.-

Health Direct Australia. (2022, May). *When to tell people you are pregnant.* Pregnancy Birth Baby. https://www.pregnancybirthbaby.o rg.au/when-to-tell-people-you-are-pregnant

Health Partners. (n.d.). *Father-baby bonding: How dads can bond with babies during pregnancy and from the moment they're born.* HealthPartners

Blog. https://www.healthpartners.com/blog/tips-for-father-baby-bondi ng/#:~:text=Massage%20your%20partner%E2%80%99s

Healthdirect Australia. (n.d.). *Baby movements during pregnancy.* Pregnancy Baby Birth. https://www.pregnancybirthbaby.org.au/baby-move ments-during-pregnancy#:~:text=the%20next%20day.-

Healthdirect Australia. (2021, October). *Antenatal classes.* Pregnancy Birth Baby. https://www.pregnancybirthbaby.org.au/antenatal-classes#: ~:text=on%20Australian%20websites-

Healthline Editorial Team. (2016, January 15). *Labor and delivery: Frequently asked questions.* Healthline. https://www.healthline.com/health /pregnancy/labor-frequently-asked-questions

Healthwise Staff. (2022, February 23). *Second-trimester fetal ultrasound: About this test.* My Health Alberta. https://myhealth.alberta.ca/health/A fterCareInformation/pages/conditions.aspx?HwId=abk7279

Healthy relationships with partners in pregnancy. (2022, November 10). Raising Children Network. https://raisingchildren.net.au/pregnancy/pregnancy-for-partners/relatio nships-and-feelings/healthy-relationships-with-partners-pregnancy#:~:te xt=strong%20and%20healthy.-

Higuera, V. (2019, December 18). *What is a babymoon and how do you plan one?* Healthline. https://www.healthline.com/health/pregnancy/ba bymoon

Higuera, V. (2020, June 18). *7 Things to consider when choosing a pediatrician.* Healthline. https://www.healthline.com/health/childrens-health/ how-to-choose-a-pediatrician#things-to-consider:~:text=1.%20Is%20the

Horsager-Boehrer, R. (2021, August 17). *1 in 10 dads experience postpartum depression, anxiety: How to spot the signs.* UTSouthwestern Medical Center. https://utswmed.org/medblog/paternal-postpartum-depression/

Hospital bag checklist—What to pack for mom, baby and partner. (2021, November 21). Pampers. https://www.pampers.com/en-us/pregnancy/giving-birth/article/what-to-pack-in-your-hospital-bag-go-bag-checklist

How common is infertility? (2018, February 8). NIH. https://www.nichd.nih.gov/health/topics/infertility/conditioninfo/common#:~:text=About%209%25%20of

How do I support my partner after a birth they found traumatic? | Labour & birth articles & support | NCT. (2022, January). NCT . https://www.nct.org.uk/labour-birth/you-after-birth/how-do-i-support-my-partner-after-birth-they-found-traumatic#:~:text=affected%20you.-

How to plan for your child's future wisely. (n.d.). PersonalFN. https://www.personalfn.com/guide/childs-future#Planning-For-Child%E2%80%99s-Education:~:text=%22Education%20is%20the

Hyperbilirubinemia in the newborn. (n.d.). University Hospitals. https://www.uhhospitals.org/rainbow/services/pediatric-neonatology/conditions-and-treatments/article/Diseases-and-Conditions---Pediatrics/hyperbilirubinemia-in-the-newborn#:~:text=What%20can%20I

Hyperbilirubinemia in the newborn . (n.d.). University Hospitals. https://www.uhhospitals.org/rainbow/services/pediatric-neonatology/conditions-and-treatments/article/Diseases-and-Conditions---Pediatrics/hyperbilirubinemia-in-the-newborn#:~:text=Hyperbilirubinemia%20in%20the

If you want to go fast, go alone. If you want to go far, go together. African Proverb. (n.d.) . Goodreads. https://www.goodreads.com/book/show/41705059-if-you-want-to-go-fast-go-alone-if-you-want-to-go-far-go-together-af

Iftikhar, N. (2020, July 31). *Emergency C-section: Why they're needed and what to expect.* Health-

line. https://www.healthline.com/health/pregnancy/emergency-c-sectio
n#definition:~:text=What%20is%20an%20emergency

Immergut, D. J. (2022, August 5). *Your baby shower etiquette guide.*
P a r e n t s .
https://www.parents.com/baby/shower/planning-a-baby-shower/a-quic
k-etiquette-guide-to-baby-celebrations/#:~:text=When%20should%20yo
u%20plan

Infertility Causes. (2020, December 14). Cleveland Clin-
ic. https://my.clevelandclinic.org/health/diseases/16083-infertility-cause
s#:~:text=What%20are%20risk%20factors%20for%20male

Kleiman, K. (2011, March 20). *For dads: What to do, what not to do when
your wife has PPD* . Psychology Today.
https://www.psychologytoday.com/za/blog/isnt-what-i-expected/20110
3/dads-what-do-what-not-do-when-your-wife-has-ppd#:~:text=Practical
%20Things%20You

Krieger, L. (2022, May 16). *9 Things to do to get your home ready before
baby comes.* Parents.
https://www.parents.com/pregnancy/my-life/preparing-for-baby/9-thing
s-to-do-to-get-your-house-in-order-before-baby-comes/#:~:text=Prepare
%20For%20Your%20Future

Labour . (n.d.). Teach Me Physiolo-
gy. https://teachmephysiology.com/reproductive-system/pregnancy/lab
our/#:~:text=Initiation%20of%20Labour

Labour and Birth. (n.d.). Healthy Parents Healthy Children. https://www.healthyparentshealthychildren.ca/im-pregnant/labo
ur-and-birth/ways-to-stay-relaxed#:~:text=Let%20go-

Lake, R. (2023, February 2). *Opening a savings account for a newborn baby:
What you need to know first.* SoFi. https://www.sofi.com/learn/content/
how-to-open-a-savings-account-for-a-baby/

List of what you DON'T need in your hospital bag. (n.d.). Emma's Diary. https://www.emmasdiary.co.uk/blog/what-you-dont-need-in-your-hospital-bag#:~:text=10%20items%20you

Lombardi, L. (2021, August 31). *Pregnancy sex through the trimesters.* What to Expect. https://www.whattoexpect.com/pregnancy/sex-and-relationships/pregnancy-sex-through-the-trimesters/

Marcin, A. (2020, May 13). *Natural ways to induce labor.* Healthline. https://www.healthline.com/health/pregnancy/natural-ways-to-induce-labor#exercise

Mayo Clinic Staff. (n.d.). *Preterm labor - Symptoms and causes.* Mayo Clinic. https://www.mayoclinic.org/diseases-conditions/preterm-labor/symptoms-causes/syc-20376842#:~:text=a%20Healthy%20Pregnancy-

Mayo Clinic Staff. (2021, October 16). *Miscarriage.* Mayo Clinic. https://www.mayoclinic.org/diseases-conditions/pregnancy-loss-miscarriage/symptoms-causes/

Mayo Clinic Staff. (2022a, January 4). *Iron deficiency anemia.* Mayo Clinic. https://www.mayoclinic.org/diseases-conditions/iron-deficiency-anemia/symptoms-causes/syc-20355034#:~:text=from%20Mayo%20Clinic-

Mayo Clinic Staff. (2022b, March 12). *Ectopic pregnancy.* Mayo Clinic. https://www.mayoclinic.org/diseases-conditions/ectopic-pregnancy/symptoms-causes/syc-20372088#:~:text=Pregnancy%20begins%20with

Mayo Clinic Staff. (2022c, April 9). *Gestational diabetes.* Mayo Clinic. https://www.mayoclinic.org/diseases-conditions/gestational-diabetes/symptoms-causes/syc-20355339#:~:text=a%20Healthy%20Pregnancy-

Mayo Clinic Staff. (2022d, July 22). *Sex during pregnancy: What's OK, what's not.* Mayo Clinic. https://www.mayoclinic.org/healthy-lifestyle/pregnancy-week-by-week/i

n - d e p t h / s e x - d u r i n g - p r e g n a n -
cy/art-20045318#:~:text=Are%20there%20times

McQueen, J. (2023, March 3). *Doctor, doula, or midwife? How to choose.*
WebMD. https://www.webmd.com/baby/guide/doctor-doula-midwif
e#:~:text=s%20birth%20plan.-

Mehta, P. (n.d.). *What to know about the best time to get an epidural.*
WebMD. https://www.webmd.com/baby/what-to-know-best-time-to
-get-epidural#:~:text=having%20an%20epidural.-

Metzger, G. K. (2022, August 9). *Pregnancy glossary.* WebMD. https:/
/www.webmd.com/baby/pregnancy-glossary

Mucus   plug.   (2021,   July   6).   Cleveland   Clinic. https://my.clevelandclinic.org/health/symptoms/21606-mucus-pl
ug#:~:text=When%20do%20you

New dads and mental health — 8 Tips to stay healthy. (2022, July 22).
Emerson Health. https://www.emersonhospital.org/articles/new-dads
-and-mental-health/

Newborn Appearance . (n.d.). University of Rochester Medical Center.
https://www.urmc.rochester.edu/encyclopedia/content.aspx?Content
TypeID=90&ContentID=P02691#:~:text=A%20baby%27s%20skin

Newborn   reflexes.   (n.d.).   Stanford   Chil-
drens. https://www.stanfordchildrens.org/en/topic/default?id=newb
orn-reflexes-90-P02630#:~:text=Suck%20reflex

Newborn screenings after childbirth. (2023). Penn Medicine Lancester
General Health. https://www.lancastergeneralhealth.org/health-hub
-home/motherhood/the-first-year/newborn-screenings-after-childbirth

NHS Choices. (n.d.). *Pregnancy FAQs.* Better Health Start for Life.
https://www.nhs.uk/start4life/pregnancy/pregnancy-faqs/

Pain relief in labour. (2023, March 13). NHS. https://www.nhs.uk/pregnancy/labour-and-birth/what-happens/pain-relief-in-labour/#:~:text=Your%20pain%20relief

ParentCo. (2017, April 6). *More than just a birth plan: Crucial questions to discuss with your partner.* ParentCo. https://www.parent.com/blogs/conversations/more-than-a-birth-plan-45-crucial-questions-to-discuss-with-partner#:~:text=In%20the%20event%20of%20the

Parents Editors. (2023, February 3). *8 Important questions to ask your pediatrician.* Parents. https://www.parents.com/baby/care/pediatricians-medicine/checklist-questions-to-ask-the-pediatrician-youre-considering/

Parker, W. (2021, September 13). *Tips for men whose partner has had a miscarriage.* Verywell Family. https://www.verywellfamily.com/dealing-with-miscarriage-1270770#:~:text=by%20his%20partner.-

Pelzer, K. (2023, March 12). *150 Best dad jokes that are so bad and so funny!* Parade. https://parade.com/940979/kelseypelzer/best-dad-jokes/

Picture Quotes. (n.d.). Picture Quotes. http://www.picturequotes.com/i-need-to-start-caring-about-myself-if-im-going-to-be-a-proper-father-quote-280776

Pinchin, K. (2019, May 10). *25 things to talk about before getting pregnant.* Today's Parent. https://www.todaysparent.com/getting-pregnant/things-to-talk-about-before-getting-pregnant/

Placental abruption. (n.d.). Mayo Clinic. https://www.mayoclinic.org/diseases-conditions/placental-abruption/symptoms-causes/syc-20376458#:~:text=Placental%20abruption%20

Prasertong, A. (2020, September 30). *5 Dos & don'ts for freezing meals before baby arrives.* Kitchn. https://www.thekitchn.com/5-dos-donts-for-freezing-meals-before-baby-arrives-216363

Preeclampsia. (n.d.). Mayo Clin-
ic. https://www.mayoclinic.org/diseases-conditions/preeclampsia/symp
toms-causes/syc-20355745#:~:text=a%20Healthy%20Pregnancy-

Pregnancy week by week. (n.d.). Flo Health. https://flo.health/pregnancy
/week-by-week

Prenatal couple yoga & its benefits. (2019, September). Beauty Mums &
Babies. https://beautymumsbabies.com/pregnancy/prenatal-couple-yog
a-its-benefits/#:~:text=Prenatal%20couple%20yoga%20encourages

Prenatal genetic screening tests. (2021, December).
ACOG. https://www.acog.org/womens-health/faqs/prenatal-genetic-sc
reening-tests#:~:text=Second%2Dtrimester%20screening%20includes

Proper storage and preparation of breast milk. (2022,
January 24). Centers for Disease Control and Prevention. https://www.cdc.gov/breastfeeding/recommendations/handling_
breastmilk.htm#:~:text=Top%20of%20Page-

Ramasamy, R., Schulster, M., & Bernie, A. (2016). The role of estradiol
in male reproductive function. *Asian Journal of Andrology*, *18*(3), 435.
https://doi.org/10.4103/1008-682x.173932

*Reaching out to other dads for support during pregnancy and beyond |
Tommy's*. (n.d.). Tommys.
https://www.tommys.org/pregnancy-information/news-and-blogs/reach
ing-out-other-dads-support-during-pregnancy-and-beyond#:~:text=Man
aging%20mental%20health

Recovering from delivery (Postpartum recovery). (2020, August 28). Family Doctor. https://familydoctor.org/recovering-from-delivery/#:~:text=
Your%20delivery%20may

Relationship problems and pregnancy. (n.d.). Tommy's.
https://www.tommys.org/pregnancy-information/im-pregnant/mental

-wellbeing/relationship-problems-and-pregnancy#:~:text=Why%20supp
ortive%20relationships

Rodgers,   L.   (2022a,   May   18).   *How   to   support   your   partner   during   pregnancy*.   What   to   Expect. https://www.whattoexpect.com/pregnancy/dads-guide/support-p
artner-during-pregnancy/#:~:text=Shoulder%20more%20than

Rodgers,   L.   (2022b,   June   13).   *Week-by-week   pregnancy   advice   for   expecting   dads   and   partners*.   What   to   Expect. https://www.whattoexpect.com/pregnancy/for-dad/week-by-week
-pregnancy-advice-dads-partners/#:~:text=Week%2014

Scherer, Z. (2021, September 16). *College-educated women and non-his-
panic white women more likely to work during first pregnancy*. The United
States Census Bureau. https://www.census.gov/library/stories/2021/09
/two-thirds-recent-first-time-fathers-took-time-off-after-birth.html

Smith, L. (2018, March 12). *Your pregnancy at 14 weeks*. Medical
News Today. https://www.medicalnewstoday.com/articles/300223#thi
ngs-to-do

Smith, V. (n.d.). *55+ adorable dad to be quotes*. The Mummy Bubble.
https://themummybubble.co.uk/dad-to-be-quotes/

Stages   of   labour.   (n.d.).   Tommys. https://www.tommys.org/pregnancy-information/giving-birth/sta
ges-labour#:~:text=Before%20labour%20gets

Symphysis   Pubis   Dysfunction.   (n.d.).   Cleveland   Clinic. https://my.clevelandclinic.org/health/diseases/22122-symphysis-pubi
s-dysfunction#:~:text=What%20is%20symphysis

Tay-Sachs disease: Symptoms, cause, treatment. (2020, December 18).
Cleveland Clinic. https://my.clevelandclinic.org/health/diseases/14348
-tay-sachs-disease#:~:text=How%20common%20is%20Tay%2DSachs

Thakur, S. (2023, March 14). *101 Funny pregnancy quotes*. Mom Junction. https://www.momjunction.com/articles/funny-pregnanc y-quotes_00474509/#funny-pregnancy-quotes-for-dad/

Things to consider before having a baby. (n.d.). Wakemed. https://www.wakemed.org/care-and-services/womens/pregnancy-and -childbirth/pregnancy-and-childbirth-resources/educational-resource s/things-to-consider-before-having-a-baby#:~:text=Financial%20Asp ects%20to%20Planning

Third trimester. (n.d.). Stanford Medicine. https://www.stanfordchildrens.org/en/topic/default?id=third-trimes ter-85-P01242#:~:text=Fetal%20development%20during%20the%20t hird%20trimester

3 Reasons you should go on a hospital tour. (2018, April 11). St. Lukes Health. https://www.stlukeshealth.org/resources/3-reasons-you-sho uld-go-hospital-tour#:~:text=Reason%20%231%3A%20Find

20-Week screening scan. (2021, April 7). NHS. https://www.nhs.uk/pregnancy/your-pregnancy-care/20-wee k-scan/#:~:text=What%20does%20the

25 Baby girl quotes to celebrate your bundle of joy. (2023, January 20). Southern Living. https://www.southernliving.com/culture/baby-gir l-quotes

36 Questions to ask your partner before having kids. (n.d.). The Longest Shortest Time. https://longestshortesttime.com/wp-content/upload s/2018/06/36QsfromLST.pdf

Umbilical cord care in newborns. (n.d.). Mount Sinai. https://www.mountsinai.org/health-library/special-topic/um bilical-cord-care-in-newborns#:~:text=Information

WebMD Editorial Contributors. (2021, March 4). *Is it safe to use Pitocin® to induce labor?* WebMD. https://www.webmd.com/baby/is-it-safe-to-use-pitocin-to-induce-labor#:~:text=up%20the%20process.-

What are some common complications of pregnancy? (2021 20). NICHD. https://www.nichd.nih.gov/health/topics/pregnancy/conditioninfo/complications#:~:text=High%20blood%20pressure%2C%20also

What is stillbirth? (2022, September 29). Centers for Disease Control and Prevention. https://www.cdc.gov/ncbddd/stillbirth/facts.html#:~:text=Stillbirth%20is%20further%20classified

What to Expect Editors. (2021, November 16). *Pregnancy glossary*. What to Expect. https://www.whattoexpect.com/pregnancy/glossary

When to go to the hospital for childbirth. (n.d.). UCSan Diego Health. https://health.ucsd.edu/care/pregnancy-birth/hospital-stay/when-to-go/#:~:text=How%20to%20Know

Willets, M. (2023, January 19). *"The parent test" pits parenting styles against one another. So, what are the styles?* Distractify. https://www.distractify.com/p/the-parent-test-parenting-styles#:~:text=Disciplined%20%E2%80%94%20This%20approach

You and your baby at 37 weeks pregnant. (2021, October 13). NHS. https://www.nhs.uk/pregnancy/week-by-week/28-to-40-plus/37-weeks/#:~:text=37%20weeks%20pregnant-

You must do this if you are vomiting during pregnancy. (n.d.). Goodonya. https://goodonyaorganic.com/blogs/goodonya-hydrate/you-must-do-this-if-you-are-vomiting-during-pregnancy#:~:text=TIPS%20FOR%20MANAGING

Your newborn: Bringing baby home. (2021, August). Caring for Kids. https://caringforkids.cps.ca/handouts/pregnancy-and-babies/bringing_baby_home#:~:text=Copy%20Link-

www.ingramcontent.com/pod-product-compliance
Lightning Source LLC
Chambersburg PA
CBHW061152120626
46546CB00005B/2026